How English Teachers
Get Taught

CEE Monographs
Conference on English Education

The Conference on English Education is the organization within the National Council of Teachers of English most centrally concerned with the preservice and inservice education of English language arts teachers. Through this series of monographs, CEE encourages discussion of critical issues in the professional development of literacy educators, including theory, policy, research, practice, and innovation.

How English Teachers Get Taught

Methods of Teaching the Methods Class

Peter Smagorinsky
University of Oklahoma

Melissa E. Whiting
University of Oklahoma

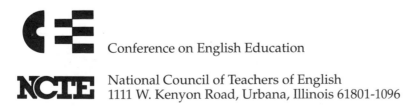

Conference on English Education

National Council of Teachers of English
1111 W. Kenyon Road, Urbana, Illinois 61801-1096

Manuscript Editors: Robert A. Heister, Hamish D. Glenn
Humanities & Sciences Associates

Production Editor: Michael G. Ryan

Interior Design: Doug Burnett

Cover Design: Barbara Yale-Read

NCTE Stock Number: 21500–3050

Grateful acknowledgment is expressed to professors Bruce C. Appleby, Helen Dale, Thomas Philion, Robert E. Probst, and Michael W. Smith for their permission to reproduce their syllabi material in this book. The syllabi are the sole property of their respective authors, and neither NCTE nor the authors of this book make claim to the copyright of those materials.

It is the policy of NCTE in its journals and other publications to provide a forum for the open discussion of ideas concerning the content and the teaching of English and the language arts. Publicity accorded to any particular point of view does not imply endorsement by the Executive Committee, the Board of Directors, or the membership at large, except in announcements of policy, where such endorsement is clearly specified.

Library of Congress Cataloging-in-Publication Data

Smagorinsky, Peter.
     How English teachers get taught : methods of teaching the methods class / Peter Smagorinsky, Melissa E. Whiting.
         p.   cm.
     Includes bibliographical references (p.) and index.
     ISBN 0-8141-2150-0
     1. English philology—Study and teaching—United States—Methodology. 2. English philology—Study and teaching (Higher)—United States. 3. English teachers—United States—training of. 4. Language arts—Methodology.   I. Whiting, Melissa E. II. Title.
PE68.U5S63 1994
420'.71'173—dc20   94-46611
                                               CIP

Dedicated to those who teach—

Contents

Acknowledgments

We would like to thank a number of people whose contributions enabled us to complete this project. First of all, we would like to thank those who sent us their methods course syllabi. Without the syllabi, we would have no book.

We would also like to thank some friends for their suggestions at various points in the development of this project. Russ Durst gave valuable advice on how to solicit the syllabi. Betsy Kahn and Larry Johannessen read the entire manuscript and gave valuable suggestions on how to improve it. Bruce Appleby read a condensed version of the manuscript and suggested some sources to investigate to provide a better rationale.

We would also like to thank Harvey Daniels for his excellent work in coordinating the review process and giving valuable suggestions on revising the manuscript we originally submitted to NCTE. Thanks are due as well to the external reviewers who contributed their professional time and wisdom to provide critiques of the original manuscript.

Finally, we would like to thank those friends and colleagues who have participated in teacher education over the years, particularly those with whom we have shared ideas and discussed pedagogy. We would single out George Hillocks, Jr., whose MAT program at the University of Chicago is an outstanding model for preparing preservice teachers for a career in education.

This project was supported by a Junior Faculty Summer Research Fellowship from the University of Oklahoma. We hope that the results have justified the investment.

Peter Smagorinsky

Melissa E. Whiting

1 Introduction

The quality and process of education have been national concerns not just in recent history, but throughout the history of schooling in America (Applebee, 1974; Kaestle, 1983; Tyack, 1974). Most citizens, critics, and reformers have focused their attention on elementary and secondary public education, with alarms, reports, and panaceas issued routinely. Among educators themselves and at times among the general public, the ways in which teachers themselves are taught have been a concern, though not one that has commanded great resources or gathered great momentum. At ten-year intervals, NCTE has issued a set of guidelines for the preparation of preservice English teachers, the latest having appeared in 1986 (Wolfe, 1986) and the next one currently under development. The Holmes Group has released several documents that have attempted to set a broad agenda for schools of education in terms of teacher preparation. The specter of NCATE follows every teacher education program with its seemingly ubiquitous program reviews. And our reading of the local newspapers tells us that many citizens are concerned about teacher preparation, particularly the ways in which tomorrow's teachers are getting indoctrinated in "politically correct" thinking at the expense of "tradition" and "the basics."

Of particular interest to English educators—and the secondary schools that hire their graduates—should be the question: How are preservice English teachers being prepared for their professional lives? We have surprisingly little knowledge about the manner in which students in methods classes are taught. An ERIC search that combined such terms as "syllabus," "language arts," and "methods class" turned up no research on the ways in which "the methods class" is taught to preservice teachers. Teaching the secondary English methods class has often been the subject of discussion (e.g., Stryker, 1967), with a strand annually devoted to the Conference on English Education (CEE) at NCTE's Spring Conference. Yet a review of Spring Conference catalogues from 1984–1993 revealed that even though many presentations have focused on the teaching of the methods class, no one has yet investigated on a wide scale how such courses are taught. English education, like the profession as a whole, appears to possess "little knowledge of what teacher education courses are currently like" (Zeichner, 1988, p. 22; cf. Feiman-Nemser, 1983).

The types of issues discussed through the CEE programs reveal a persistent interest among teacher educators about the ways in which they prepare and teach their courses. Even beyond the formal sessions, we discuss the ways in which we prepare teachers. Over dinner and in the corridors we talk about what books we use, what activities we involve students in, how we assess their progress, and other aspects of preservice education. Yet our knowledge has always been informal, much like the "lore" North (1987) has described to characterize the ways in which many teachers of writing learn their craft:

> It is driven, first, by a pragmatic logic: It is concerned with what has worked, is working, or might work in teaching, doing, or learning. . . . Second, its structure is essentially experiential. That is, the traditions, practices, and beliefs of which it is constituted are best understood as being organized within an experience-based framework: I will create my version of lore out of what has worked or might work—either in my own experience or in that of others—and I will understand and order it in terms of the circumstances under which it did so. (p. 23)

If our ERIC search, analysis of CEE programs, and experiences as consumers of scholarship are accurate, and if our experiences as practitioners of the methods class are typical, then North's characterization of the lore of composition instruction applies quite accurately to the ways in which college professors learn how to teach the methods class. With little formal knowledge of how preservice teachers are educated, all we have left to fall back on is our own experience in teaching the course and our shared conversations with peers about how we go about our business.

While this approach is serviceable to some extent, it does not provide much help for those who do not have travel allowances and therefore rarely engage in such conversations, those whose conversations are conducted among colleagues whose practices are similar to begin with, those who are designing methods courses for the first time, or those who simply want to know what is potentially available to them in teaching a methods class. In order to get a preliminary understanding of how the *undergraduate secondary English methods course* is taught, we have undertaken in this book an examination of course syllabi from as wide a range of public universities as possible to look at the ways in which English educators across the country organize a methods class, to find out what books students are reading, to see what types of activities and assessments students are engaged in, and generally to present a description of what types of experiences preservice teachers are having prior to going into their student teaching and subsequent teaching careers. By providing this account, we hope to broaden the knowledge of those who teach such courses as to the range of potential of different approaches for preparing preservice teachers.

We wish to emphasize that we understand the serious limitations of our project, the most important being that we are not examining actual programs and the real experiences that teachers and students have with them, as Grossman (1990) did in her ethnographic study of preservice teaching programs. Also, we are not examining the specific context in which programs are enacted; we have collected little information regarding the ways in which the undergraduate methods classes are situated in an overall teacher education program, or the ways in which local circumstances constrain how such courses can be taught. We also do not have access to the quality of the instruction in the classrooms themselves, in that we are not examining classes, interviewing students or instructors, or examining the changes that take place among students during the course of instruction. The window through which we look into the interior of the methods course prevents us from seeing much about the teaching of the course, including such matters as how teachers and students go about negotiating the content and process of instruction and learning.

Our window does, however, enable us to describe much about this course—enough to fill a book. Broadly speaking, we intend for our analysis of the syllabi to generate some initial knowledge about methods courses. Through this initial knowledge we hope to accomplish several goals. First of all, we want to describe the general approaches to teaching the course, the means of assessment, the types of activities, and the theoretical orientations that are being used in a number of courses across the nation. This general description should help provide a framework for further discussion of issues. We wish to use this description in order to provide English educators with possible ways in which they can prepare their undergraduate secondary English methods courses. We also hope to provide the foundation for future discussion of how English educators teach the methods course. Our analysis of the syllabi necessarily involves the imposition of our own perspective on the matter; as Hillocks (1994) has argued, even the most objective observer perceives the object of study through some sort of bias, no matter how principled or well articulated. Undoubtedly, some readers will disagree with some of our decisions, as our editor did with our original classification of one of his books. We hope, however, that in presenting our categories and judgments, we account for ourselves clearly enough so that even those who disagree with us at least see the rationale behind our decisions. Our purpose is not to have the final word in the discussion about the methods class, but rather to provide some grounds for what we hope is a healthy, spirited, and necessary professional conversation.

Although our primary goal in analyzing the syllabi is to be descriptive, inevitably we are evaluative. In discussing the implications of different ways of preparing a methods class, we have developed criteria for evaluating the potential implications of the different approaches. The criteria that we use are often consonant with both the NCTE guidelines for teacher education programs (Wolfe, 1986) and the very theories that motivate the methods courses themselves (see chapter 4). The NCTE guidelines, which we will refer to throughout this report, stress that programs in English education should foster a belief in student-centered classrooms, take a holistic perspective on teaching and learning, provide students with copious field-based experiences, focus on the needs of preservice (as opposed to in-service) teachers, model for students the effective teaching methods promoted in the course, provide experience in the analysis of effective teaching, and provide experience in the observation and practice of effective teaching. As we will explain in later chapters, we agree with these principles (although we feel the need to clarify the meaning we associate with such amorphous terms as "student-centered" and "holistic") and have generated additional criteria of our own to create a perspective for viewing the different ways of teaching the methods course.

While we are not concerned with finding the "best" way to teach a methods course, we are concerned with describing ways in which it can be effectively taught. We hope that our analysis of the methods course syllabi provides some understanding of the potential for developing instruction that facilitates learning among preservice teachers.

How We Analyzed the Syllabi

We next explain the way in which we gathered and analyzed the syllabi, an account that should help illuminate some of the processes we went through in deciding what to examine in the syllabi and how to report what we found. At the beginning of the winter and fall terms of 1992, we sent letters to instructors of undergraduate secondary English methods courses at over three hundred public universities in the United States, requesting that they send us their methods course syllabi. The universities we contacted represented a cross-section of state universities, including large research universities, smaller regional colleges and universities, city colleges, and traditionally black universities. We received a total of eighty-one syllabi, including more than one from some universities in which two professors taught the course. Appendix B provides a list of all universities contributing syllabi.

We know of two specific reasons why fewer than one-third of the recipients of the letter sent us their syllabi, and a third reason which we suspect, but cannot substantiate. The first reason that some universities did not provide syllabi was revealed in a few letters we received saying that the university in question had no English education program or taught no specific course in secondary English methods; we can assume that they are representative of other such situations from which we got no reply.

We received evidence of a second reason through an eloquent letter written by a professor who explained why he had decided not to participate, an account that we fear may be representative of the attitude many academics have toward one another's motives:

> I have decided not to accede to your request to send you material describing the course I teach in English methods. . . . Somewhere in *Biographia Literaria* Coleridge says that the medium through which angels communicate with each other is the freedom which they have in common. Although Coleridge's conclusion was a deduction from theological doctrines, sufficiently arcane, specific to the being of angels, on obvious grounds he might have said the very same thing about humans. When one suspects that certain others will not take one's statements at their plain face value but instead torture them into a code signifying something else, then one is inclined to guard one's meanings and not willingly allow those others to paraphrase or summarize them. . . . Since you and I are not acquainted, I can feel no assurance that we share that freedom through which humans as well as angels communicate with each other.

We hope that our report on the syllabi does not further substantiate this professor's distrust of academic inquiry.

The third reason is that some people just never seem to respond to surveys, publishers' sweepstakes, or other solicitations they find in their mailboxes. We suspect that many of our nonrespondents fell into this last category.

We read each syllabus five times. For the first reading, each of us read the complete stack of syllabi separately to gather initial impressions regarding their overall structure, the books read, the types of assignments required, and whatever other information the syllabi revealed about the content and method of the course. During this reading we took one formal count, that being the frequency with which individual textbooks appeared on the syllabi. By initially assembling a list of the textbooks used, we could begin acquiring the books to read and evaluate as we continued our analysis of the syllabi themselves.

The remaining four readings of the syllabi came through collaborative analysis. We decided to analyze them through conversation because our discussion of the syllabi was crucial to the development of our insights. Through our discussion we tried to understand the instructional approach, content, and processes of the courses and how that information could be helpful to those designing methods classes for their own students.

Our initial reading of the syllabi suggested to us that we should focus next on three features: the instructional approaches of the syllabi, the activities through which students were evaluated, and the extent to which the syllabi included a field-experience component. In that the identification of the instructional approaches would be a subjective judgment, we decided that in our second reading of the syllabi we would generate preliminary categories that we would refine in later readings. The types of activities used for evaluation and the presence of a field-experience component were more amenable to quick agreement, and so we tabulated them during the second reading.

The third reading of the syllabi was focused exclusively on categorizing their instructional approaches. During our first two readings, we had identified a great many possible categories and jotted down characteristics of each category we had identified. During our third reading of the syllabi, we determined the final categories and classified each syllabus according to its instructional approach.

Our fourth reading of the syllabi was focused on two areas: determining the extent to which a course attempted to situate the students' coursework in some sort of practical experience, and determining the extent to which a course encouraged or required collaboration on the part of students. The decision to focus on these areas came about through questions developed during the first three readings of the syllabi and through our ongoing reading of both the texts required in the courses and the NCTE guidelines (Wolfe, 1986) for teacher preparation. All seemed to stress the need to connect life in the classroom with "real" life experiences and all encouraged collaborative learning. We wanted to see, therefore, the extent to which the courses themselves required such participation.

The fifth reading of the syllabi focused on the extent to which the syllabi had been influenced by the NCTE guidelines. We had initially noted references to the guidelines in a few syllabi and began to see through repeated readings the ways in which the NCTE guidelines had influenced them. In our fifth reading, we also cleared up loose ends and made final decisions about how we would prepare our manuscript in response to what we had seen in the syllabi.

The collaborative readings of the syllabi took place in focused two- to three-hour sessions. We spent the rest of our time reading and discussing the textbooks to prepare the section on the theories that undergird the courses; reading NCTE, NCATE, and Holmes Group publications to see if we could find policies influencing syllabus development; chasing down obscure references to the texts used in the syllabi; and discussing the possible ways in which we could organize and explain the types of assignments required on the syllabi, the types of collaboration we found, and any other ideas and insights we developed through our analysis and discussion. The process of analysis was developed through what the syllabi and their implications revealed to us, and this process was continually influenced by other ideas we developed in our independent and collaborative consideration of the syllabi. The actual writing of the manuscript began to take place during these conversations, with one of us at the word processor and each of us with a stack of syllabi and our various drafts, lists, and books, discussing possible ways to analyze the syllabi even as we created drafts of different sections of the report. The preparation of one section—including the discussion of what to report and the preliminary drafting itself— often helped illuminate other problems we found with the analysis of other sections, and so helped us develop insights as to how to proceed next. The process of analyzing the syllabi, therefore, was very important to the ways in which we thought about the syllabi and prepared the final report.

The next three chapters report what we found in the syllabi. We begin with an account of the five primary approaches taken by teachers of the methods course to engage students in the process of learning their trade.

2 Approaches to Teaching the Methods Class

The eighty-one universities that responded to our solicitation contributed close to one hundred syllabi, with some universities sending syllabi from more than one instructor. Seventy-nine of the syllabi were for a course that we could agree served as a "methods class." We identified a course as a "methods course" through the appearance of some combination of a cover letter from the instructor labeling it as such, the course title itself (i.e., "Methods of Teaching Secondary English"), the materials read (such as a textbook about teaching secondary English), and the issues covered (the teaching of writing, literature, and language).

Of syllabi identified as methods classes, three were too skeletal to classify, offering only a list of topics to be covered with no additional information, and so were not included in the analysis. Several instructors also included other course syllabi with the explanation that their programs required not just a methods class, but a series of courses that included classes in young adult literature, composition instruction, language study, and/or language arts curriculum. For a few universities, a series of such courses actually took the place of the methods course; rather than taking a single course in teaching methods, the students would take two or three courses that focused separately on literature, writing, language, and perhaps some other strand of language arts.

For the analysis we conducted on the remaining syllabi, we decided to focus only on those courses that we had labeled as "methods courses." We focused on the methods class because the other types of classes had a much more specific purpose and so tended to approach the topics and material differently. A course in teaching writing did not necessarily need to be concerned about the relationship between teaching literature and writing, about the uses of drama, about classroom management, and about other aspects of teaching often found in a teaching methods class; several courses in the teaching of writing served more as writing workshops than as courses in how to teach English. Courses in young adult literature often did not include books about teaching methods, instead involving students in the reading of a great deal of adolescent literature. While we admired many of these courses, we decided that their overall purpose—and therefore their approach—was different from that of the methods course and thus decided not to include them in our analysis. We report information from these other syllabi in chapter 4, "Theories and Issues Represented in Syllabi," where we report on the texts read by preservice English teachers.

What follows is our classification of the methods course syllabi. We found that courses took one (or more) of the following approaches: *survey, workshop, experience-based, reflective,* and *theoretical,* with some syllabi receiving two labels because of their dual focus. Table 1 shows how many syllabi of each type we identified. We should stress that our identification of a course in a particular category was not always an obvious decision; at times we would classify a course because it was closer to one category than to another, rather than because it met all of the criteria we had established. The frequency with which we identified each type of course, then, should be taken as a rough indicator rather than a precise figure of how many such courses we found.

As table 1 reveals, some courses included a practicum. We received a total of six syllabi that either included a separate syllabus for a practicum or made reference to a practicum. In that we did not request a practicum syllabus, we do not know the extent to which practica are paired with methods courses. Practicum syllabi were not included in the analysis of the approaches to teaching the methods class.

Following is an account of each type of approach we identified in the syllabi, along with illustrations of activities and processes that characterized them. After our review of the syllabi, we provide a discussion of the consequences of the different approaches to teaching the course, based on criteria we suggest for planning a methods class.

The Survey Approach

Some syllabi identified themselves in their course description as a survey of issues relevant to the teaching of secondary English. We found that many other syllabi took a survey approach as well. A survey course attempts to cover a great many issues and topics during a single semester. One characteristic of a survey course is that the class sessions can be taught in almost any order; the knowledge from one session to another does not build toward a synthesis, but tends to move from topic to topic.

Survey courses often follow the organization of a single textbook, starting out with a historical perspective and then moving on to cover a series of topics in discrete class sessions. Survey courses cover grammar, computers, writing, testing and evaluation, debate, discipline, classroom management, learning styles, objectives, lesson plans, units, the research paper, school law, exceptional learners, multi-ethnic learners, and other topics, with one topic or a cluster of topics covered in a single session. Often, the classes are taught by a series of guest speakers, again contributing to a sense of separation from class to class. A survey approach seems to assume that a student can build knowledge about teaching from parts to whole; that is, that the coverage of a great many issues will result in an aggregate understanding of the whole of teaching.

Survey courses tend to require students to do a great many brief assignments, such as writing lesson plans and abstracts of articles, and have few or no extended assignments that require synthesis. They often include midterm and final exams, although the content of those exams was not revealed in the syllabi. When students are required to write an instructional unit, the unit tends to be short, from five to ten days in length, or of an unspecified length.

Simply stated, surveys attempt to cover all the bases. Often, a survey syllabus would begin with a catalogue-style course description and then present the students with a lengthy list of course objectives or outcomes. The list of objectives often extended for up to three single-spaced pages, covering virtually every responsibility a teacher could have in a classroom, school, and professional community. The objectives were usually presented in an extensive outline form, stated in precise, detached, and technical language such as "Identify directed reading activities appropriate for given reading objectives." Often, the objectives referred to goals that were extraordinarily complex and might

Table 1. Classification of the methods course syllabi.

Type of approach	Number of syllabi reflecting approach
Survey	27
Workshop	23
Experience-based	8
Theoretical	4
Reflective	2
Reflective/Workshop	5
Reflective/Experienced-based	3
Workshop with practicum	2
Other practica included	4

require a complete reorientation on the part of preservice teachers, such as "Explain the interdependence needed among the various cultures for the enhancement of learning how to function and learn in a pluralistic society." Frequently, we couldn't tell from further study of the content of the class sessions just how the course would help the students meet the many and varied objectives and outcomes presented at the beginning of the syllabus.

As we read these lengthy lists of objectives, we often found ourselves overwhelmed by the extraordinary range and scope of expectations preservice teachers were presented with at the front end of the syllabus. Each author of this report has taught for over a decade in public school classes and still found the lists to be quite daunting. We wondered how preservice teachers would feel upon being presented with such an ambitious—and often forbidding—set of objectives as their introduction to the methods class.

The goal of a survey course appears to be to provide preservice teachers with an introduction to as broad a range of issues as possible prior to their entry into the field. The advantage of such an approach is that students will be exposed to a range of topics that will ultimately affect them in their careers.

The survey approach appears to have more potential disadvantages than advantages. As we read through many syllabi taking this approach, we wondered whether such syllabi might be attempting to satisfy all of the requirements set forth by NCTE in its *Guidelines for the Preparation of Teachers of English Language Arts* (Wolfe, 1986), as well as the demands of other institutional sources (such as state departments of education with their learner outcomes and other mandates) by identifying the vast array of professional qualities expected of a teacher, all in a single course. The assumption seems to be that an understanding of the many parts will lead to a grasp of the whole. In attempting to set broad goals, survey courses often neglected to engage students in the processes of connecting knowledge and integrating understandings that strike us as being the heart and soul of NCTE's 1986 recommendations, which stress an emphasis on student-centered classrooms, the need for a holistic perspective on learning, and the need to situate learning about teaching in real teaching environments. Survey courses represented the "coverage" approach that we suspect the authors of the NCTE report would advise against, and mitigate the likelihood that the course will be process-oriented, interactive, integrated, and have other qualities central to the spirit of the guidelines. As we will discuss in our analysis of other types of course arrangements, the potential for learning about teaching seems much greater when a course has a more specific focus and strives for fewer, more reachable goals.

The Workshop Approach

A workshop consistently devotes class sessions to students' participation in the activities they are being taught to teach. A workshop might involve class sessions devoted to small-group development of lesson plans, assessments, prereading activities, and other practical teaching activities; in-class collaborative activities are a central means of learning in a workshop.

A workshop tends to sequence class sessions so that the material studied in each class develops understandings from prior learning and is important to the understanding of what follows. There is continuity among classes and a building toward a concrete, synthesizing goal. That goal is often realized in a large project such as a portfolio or the development of an extended instructional unit of four to six weeks that incorporates all of the planning strategies learned throughout the course.

The class tends to build from whole to parts; in other words, all assignments and activities are situated in the context of a larger plan. Literature, composition, grammar, and other topics covered tend to be integrated rather than be covered in discrete sessions, as happens in a survey course. A workshop is recursive in its coverage of issues; students work on developing units and/or lessons in successive class sessions, often using class time to critique and revise work done in previous classes. As one syllabus informed the students, "Because revision and rereading are essential aspects of writing and reading, regard all work as in progress."

Often, students work on lessons and units with partners or in small collaborative groups, both in class and in the development of outside projects. Both students and teachers act as critics of ongoing class projects. Students often engage in teaching demonstrations of lessons they have developed in their workshop activities, with feedback from classmates and their instructor. A workshop attempts to move from theory to practice in a "hands-on" fashion with an emphasis on continuity, feedback, and revision.

We will offer one example of how a workshop attempts to integrate all of the parts of teaching into a coherent whole, using class sessions for collaborative planning and feedback. One course offered the following sequence of classes:

Session #6: Planning units. Read *Explorations,* chapter 3, and sample unit (in xerox packet).

Daily exercise: *Explorations,* p. 71. Start planning your unit.

Class: Discussion of criteria for good units (handout on integrated units), rubric for grading unit plans, discussion of your initial plans, evaluation of several units in groups.

Session #7: Skim *Explorations,* chapter 4. Read chapters 5 and 6. Work on unit.

Daily exercise: *Explorations,* p. 108, "Four Case Studies."

Class: Discussion of text; case study discussion; demo lessons on "WOW logs" and LTD.

Session #8: Read *Explorations,* chapters 7 and 8. Work on unit. Prepare one-page written progress report on your unit project. Focus on questions I can answer for you and problems I can help solve.

Daily exercise: Do a WOW log on these two chapters.

Class: Discussion of the log entries and the chapters, book paths; individual conferences with me on unit plans.

Session #9: Read *Explorations,* chapters 9 and 10. "Writing Strategies Guide" (in xerox packet), pages 1–16 (intro and topics 1–10). Work on unit.

Daily exercise: *Explorations,* "The Assignment Makers." Study these writing assignments and evaluate them from YOUR point of view. Take notes and be ready to report.

Class: Discussion of reading and assignments; modeling of various prewriting strategies to get your own piece of writing started. Modeling a writing instruction sequence.

Session #10: Read *Explorations,* chapters 11 and 12 and "Writing Strategies Guide," pp. 17–29 (topics 11–19). Revise your piece. Work on your unit.

Daily exercise: Keep a journal or log describing all the various mental processes and activities you go through in writing this piece. (What idea you started with, how and when you changed your mind, when you revised, and what you did, etc.).

Class: Discussion of chapters, language interludes and how they should work, DOL, and exercise. Modeling peer review, peer conferences on pieces.

Session #11: Read "Writing Strategies Guide," pp. 30–33. Complete your piece and prepare final copy of it. Work on your unit. Bring draft to class.

No daily exercise.

Class: Sharing/publication of pieces, workshop on responding to and grading student writing. Peer revision and editing on unit plan drafts.

Session #12: Complete unit plan and hand in. In class, review and
    wrap up; final exam last hour.

As this series of classes illustrates, the workshop attempts to es-
tablish continuity from class to class, involving students in the aspects
of learning (i.e., attention to the processes involved in personal writing)
that the instructor hopes to encourage them to promote among their
own students. It couples that experience with continual work on and
revision of the students' instructional units, which we gather might include the sort of attention to process modeled in the students' reflections on their developing "pieces." The sequence of classes reported
above does not include as much in-class work on planning the instructional unit as some of the other workshops we found, providing as it
does one small-group planning session in Session #6. It does, however,
reveal how the students learn from a combination of model instructional
units, instruction from the textbook, supplemental handouts on unit
design (i.e., the criteria and rubric), in-process progress reports and feedback, and the final sharing of finished products. This series of classes
provides a good illustration of the ways in which a workshop can help
students synthesize knowledge from a number of different areas and
work over time to develop a single, extended project with in-process
instruction and feedback on its development from the instructor and
classmates.

The major underlying assumption of a workshop approach is that
a single course is insufficient for preparing students for all professional
responsibilities and that students benefit from learning a few specific
processes well, rather than being exposed to a large number of issues.
In order to learn these specific processes, students need to engage in
extended process-oriented work that frequently cycles back to previously learned knowledge of content and procedure. Workshops assume
that students learn from doing "hands-on" work through collaborative
activities.

An advantage of the workshop approach is that students learn in
an environment that models many of the teaching and learning strategies advocated in course texts (i.e., collaborative, process-oriented, holistic learning). The students tend to produce work that is practical; that
is, the lessons they design and share with one another may ultimately
be used in their teaching (ideally their student teaching). Students tend
to learn one teaching approach very well through their extended work
at developing lessons and units.

Workshops are potentially problematic, too. In focusing on a particular teaching method, students may emerge with a somewhat paro-

chial attitude about how to teach, one that may be at odds with the pedagogy practiced by their cooperating teachers and by the teachers in the district they ultimately work in. Workshops also may operate in a "best-of-all-possible-worlds" environment, with lessons designed but not tested in "real world" conditions; students may be unprepared for the harsh reality of students who don't do the activities or assignments that appear so worthwhile in a lesson or unit plan. Instructors who approach the methods course through a workshop approach need to caution students about the availability of methods other than the ones learned in the methods class, and to advise them of the likelihood that a unit works much better in theory than it does in practice.

The Experience-Based Approach

An experience-based course deliberately links theory and practice, usually through extensive observations of secondary English classrooms and often by requiring preservice teachers to both plan instruction with and teach in the classes of secondary school teachers. One experience-based course listed the following objectives as the very first item on its syllabus:

> To provide adequate field experience which links theory and practice; to provide a screening mechanism for entrance into student teaching; to introduce undergraduates to public schools and their language arts curricula.

Experience-based classes typically alternate between field experience and regular class sessions, with the regular sessions consisting of discussions of reading assignments, shared observations from field experiences, planning of instruction, and teaching demonstrations.

One experience-based course illustrates well the way in which field experience can make up a central part of the course. The class met for the first three weeks in regular sessions, engaging in the reading and discussion of issues from the course texts. Weeks four through seven were spent in schools in order to give the students, as the syllabus said, "uninterrupted time for observations in the schools. This will allow you to observe several classes a day, five days a week, which will give you a somewhat more coherent picture of teaching than you would otherwise get." Weeks eight and nine marked a return to the classroom, where students made presentations on lessons they had developed during their field observations, getting feedback from the instructor and classmates. The final week of the term was devoted to a final exam and wrap-up of the course.

Class time in experience-based courses was often devoted to the planning and demonstration of lessons and units. One syllabus informed the students of the ways in which they would use class time to learn about the practice of teaching:

> Much of our class time will be spent in discussion of your reading, but we will also experiment with some of the techniques the texts and articles will recommend. It will be an imprecise simulation at best, but lacking the opportunity to bring a high school group into the classroom, we will have to satisfy ourselves at first with some practice within our own group. These trial runs will be opportunities to experiment within a group that ought to be encouraging and supportive. For those of us beginning teaching, they will be opportunities to have a fairly comfortable experience controlling a group and instructing, and for those of us who have taught before, they may be chances to try out ideas, perhaps to experiment with techniques or content.

Another syllabus was organized so that the students met for regular one-hour sessions in the morning and then returned for a two-hour "lab" in the afternoon. Each lab session had a specific instructional purpose, such as "lesson-planning work sessions" and "microteaching [on] student response to literature." Following ten weeks of this structure, the course went into a practicum; the syllabus informed the students that "during the last three weeks of the term, you will be joining with two or three other students to team-teach in a class in the [local school district]. You will be responsible for planning and teaching two to three classes in your teams." In this course, rather than having the field experience come in the middle of the course to scaffold students' design of their own lessons, the students practiced their teaching and planning first and then applied them in their practicum.

In addition to allowing students to practice their teaching, some experience-based classes include presentations by local "master teachers," a study of "cases" of problematic teaching situations, and a study of documents produced by the state department of education concerning assessment, outcomes, and other mandates. Assignments often include logs of classroom observations, lesson plans prepared under the supervision of cooperating teachers, classes taught in the classrooms of cooperating teachers, the evaluation of student writing, work as tutors in a university writing lab, participation in a roundtable discussion with local teachers and other preservice students, a written literacy profile of a secondary school student, an oral report on a classroom observation, and reflection on their field-based observations and experiences in journals.

Experience-based courses operate on the assumption that practical experience benefits preservice teachers because it teaches them the reality of the classroom. Research on teachers' knowledge supports some aspects of an experience-based approach. Lampert (1984) has determined that teachers' knowledge needs to be context-specific; that is, it must respond to the needs of specific students in particular schools and communities. An experience-based class can help preservice teachers see the ways in which a particular text or teaching approach might work well in one context but not another.

A potential problem of an experience-based methods class is that it depends in part on the quality of the teachers with whom the preservice teachers work. Some cooperating teachers are none-too-cooperative, placing preservice teachers in servile roles, providing a jaded view of the profession, imposing archaic views of students and teaching, and otherwise providing a questionable indoctrination to the world of teaching. Unsatisfying relationships with teachers in the field may discourage preservice teachers in their efforts to enter the profession. Those who teach experience-based courses need to make an effort to provide good mentoring relationships in the field and to provide counseling when the inevitable sour relationship develops.

The Theoretical Approach

A theoretical course attempts to involve students in the consideration of theoretical positions that drive classroom practice. The emphasis is on the theory rather than the practice. Thus, rather than being assessed primarily on the design of writing lesson plans and instructional units, students might write a series of essays considering the theoretical positions covered in the class. Our identification of a course as theoretical resulted from the extent to which the course assessed students according to their ability to articulate the theory relative to their ability to design instruction. One syllabus that we labeled as theoretical identified its course goals as follows:

> [This class] is designed to provide preservice teachers of English, speech, and theater with background on current theory and practice relevant to the teaching of their discipline to secondary school students. The course has four pragmatic objectives: (1) to help students plan and present lessons and units; (2) to assist students in evaluating student progress; (3) to enable students to define and defend informed positions on significant issues in the teaching of language, writing, literature, speech, theater, and mass media; and (4) to provide students with an understanding of

multicultural and exceptional student issues relevant to the teaching of English, speech, and theater.

We should stress again that our classification of a course as primarily theoretical did not mean that it did not include practical instruction in teaching or reflection in journals or logs. Rather, we labeled courses as theoretical when students were required as their primary means of assessment to state the theoretical underpinnings of instructional methods.

Theoretical courses rely on texts that present theoretical approaches to thinking about teaching, often supplementing them with articles and chapters collected in a course packet. Books with extensive attention to theory, usually written for college-level instruction (i.e., Lindemann's *A Rhetoric for Writing Teachers* [1982]), were often required reading for students in theoretical courses. In contrast, survey and workshop courses tended to assign practice-heavy general textbooks.

Students in theoretical courses, as noted, might be required to develop lesson plans and units. We found that the development of pedagogy is not the central means of assessment in theoretical courses. Students are involved more in writing research reports, developing "projects" that incorporate reports on articles from scholarly journals, writing papers on theoretical issues, and taking exams that involve essay questions.

Theoretical courses assume that understanding the theoretical underpinnings of different instructional approaches is of paramount importance for teachers, that from a strong theoretical background preservice teachers can proceed to develop sound instruction based on theoretical principles. An advantage to a theoretical approach is that teachers will enter the profession with more than a "trick bag" of teaching methods; rather, they will have an understanding of teaching and learning that can inform their decisions about how to work with students.

A potential problem with this approach is that the course will be light in practical ideas, that the theory will predominate and preservice teachers will be equipped with little in the way of actual method. Those who take a theoretical approach need to make sure that theory is tied to practice, as is illustrated in NCTE's "Theory and Research Into Practice" (TRIP) monograph series.

The Reflective Approach

A reflective course tends to involve students in consistent, formal reflection about the course readings, their own experiences as learners, and their own experiences in the course itself. Students in such classes typically keep a reading log (possibly a dialogue journal, with the respondent being a fellow student or the instructor), and might also write a literacy autobiography, keep a portfolio of their classroom production, keep a log of classes that they observe, write a memoir of educational experiences, write an essay about a favorite teacher, engage in reading that stresses the value of reflection, complete an I-Search paper, create a file of materials from the media related to educational issues, and engage in other reflective activities. Students in reflective courses, while often engaged in practical activities such as designing lessons and units, are likely to have as their primary means of assessment written work in which they reflect on how different approaches to teaching affect students.

Most of the courses that we identified as reflective required students to read materials that were either self-reflective themselves, such as Atwell's *In the Middle* (1987); concerned observation-based reflection about how classrooms work, such as Perl and Wilson's *Through Teachers' Eyes* (1986); or provided opportunities for students to reflect on the consequences of various beliefs about teaching, such as Gere, Fairbanks, Howes, Roop, and Schaafsma's *Language and Reflection* (1992). *Language and Reflection* was often used in reflective courses to help preservice teachers understand the assumptions that drive the four different approaches to teaching that Gere et al. identify: language as artifact, language as development, language as expression, and language as social construct. (We review *Language and Reflection* in greater depth in the conclusion to chapter 4).

Often the syllabi themselves revealed the instructors' own reflective tendencies. One instructor opened his syllabus with the following course description:

> I see our course as an opportunity to discuss important issues in the teaching of English—issues like creating multicultural curricula, teaching basic writers, and leading student-centered conversations. Since my own pedagogy is centered on the assumption that people learn best through classroom conversations in which they can share their opinions and learn about others, you will find yourself invited to shape with me both what issues we discuss, and how we discuss them. You therefore should expect to occupy multiple positions in our classroom environment: not only that of student and learner, but also that of teacher and researcher. In this sense, I hope to model for you a method of sharing authority in the English classroom which you might consider when you construct your own teaching philosophy.

You won't find me giving out any final solutions to the issues we choose to study; however, I don't expect you to leave our class-room empty-handed. By the end of the semester I hope that you will be able to articulate a coherent philosophy of teaching, name specific strategies that you will use in your student teaching, and possess several research questions which you hope to pursue in your first teaching situation.

The course description went on at length in the same vein, explaining the purpose of the course in terms of the instructor's own articulated philosophy about the nature of teaching and learning. In the instructor's opening statement to the students on the syllabus itself, he is modeling the type of reflection that he expects of them.

Students themselves were often required to reflect in journals. One journal assignment told the students that

A journal is informal by definition. Don't worry about spelling or other mechanical concerns. Just get your ideas down. What I'm looking for is a dialogue with you and a record of your thoughts and feelings as they develop and change. Feel free to ask me questions or direct comments my way. Don't feel you have to say what you think I want to hear. I'll read and evaluate them for content only. Honest. Grades will be based on effort and the thinking revealed.

Here the instructor reveals that she is more interested in the degree of reflection rather than the particular pedagogy adopted by the student. This focus on getting students to understand and articulate their beliefs about teaching was a hallmark of courses we identified as reflective.

Another class required students to write a reflection on each class session. The instructor informed the students that

I am not looking for summaries here. What I expect you to do is relate the content and experiences in class to your own learning and teaching. WRITING IS THINKING. I want to see your thinking in this section. I will be looking for "I" statements—"I think," "I wonder," "I remember"—that kind of thing. This is a time and place where your own opinions *really* count. BE HONEST!

Again, the purpose was to get students to reflect on the content and process of each class, rather than to report on the substance of the readings. Assignments of this sort were central to the evaluation of students in reflective courses, revealing the emphasis on considering the purposes behind teaching rather than the promotion of particular teaching approaches, as we often found happening in workshops.

A reflective course assumes that reflection on one's own experiences as a learner will help teachers understand better the ways in which their own students learn. One strength of a reflective approach is that it encourages teachers to question what they are doing in the classroom. As Feiman-Nemser and Buchmann (1985) point out, many preservice teachers become satisfied with their teaching as they master routines and become less likely to question prevailing norms of teaching and learning. In a reflective course, preservice teachers reflect on the benefits of a variety of teaching methods and choose those that best suit their own situations.

Paradoxically, a reflective approach can also be problematic. Feiman-Nemser and Buchmann (1985), while encouraging teachers to question their decisions, also conclude that without guidance, preservice teachers have trouble making the transition to pedagogical thinking. If a reflective course provides little guidance in helping students consider the benefits of different teaching approaches, the students may have difficulty understanding the pedagogical implications of the various methods.

Lortie (1975) has further found that teachers have a difficult time overcoming images from their own schooling and therefore might have a limited view of learning. Thus preservice teachers might replicate teaching methods they experienced as students without understanding their teachers' goals in using them. Similarly, Grossman and Richert (1988) have found that preservice teachers often rely on their memories of themselves as students to anticipate what their own students will be like, using "their memories of their interests and abilities in a particular subject matter to inform their knowledge of student understanding in that area" (p. 11). If teachers' experiences are quite different from those of their students, such reflection may cause them to teach in inappropriate ways. We know, for instance, many adults who were quite adept as adolescents at diagramming sentences and therefore wonder why the practice has been abandoned in modern English classes. Often, our own experiences are poor indicators of how other people learn. Those who teach reflective courses need to make preservice teachers aware that their own experiences should have a qualified influence on their teaching decisions, particularly when the students come from diverse backgrounds.

Discussion

Our review of the different approaches to teaching the undergraduate secondary English methods course is designed to present the worlds of possibility in preparing such a course, rather than to argue for a "best" way to teach it. The "best" way to teach a methods course undoubtedly comes from the context in which it is taught, including the disposition of the instructor, the way in which the course is situated in a larger teacher education program (including the program's overall ethos), the demands and interests of the local school systems, the requirements of the state, the characteristics of the students, and the other factors that constrain and empower instructors and students.

Undoubtedly, the approach used to teach a methods course is only one—and possibly not the best—sign of a course's potential for providing a good education. The people involved are what makes a program work. The best-designed, experience-based course will work poorly if the teachers in the field lack a commitment to working productively with the preservice teachers. A workshop will not achieve its goals if the students do not believe in activity-based learning, as attested to in the following excerpt from a letter which accompanied one syllabus:

> My most basic approach is that I try to model and demonstrate what it is I think the students need to learn and to understand about learning in English classes.
>
> Getting them to a metacognitive state about their own learning is where I start. This sometimes proves easy. Other times, as this semester, it's very difficult. We require a 2.50 GPA overall *and* in the major for students going into teaching high school English. The group this semester has a lower average GPA than I'm used to. They truly view learning as a passive activity and don't think that HOW one teaches makes a lot of difference. It's been a long time since I've had a methods class like this. I'm considering it a challenge.

This instructor's thoughts confirm what all teachers know about teaching, that the best laid plans of mice and educators can go awry if the people involved will not cooperate. The instructional approaches that we discuss, then, are necessarily somewhat limited in that they do not take into consideration the real problems that come with working with real people.

Nonetheless, we would like to set up some criteria for considering the potential effectiveness of different approaches to teaching the methods class. We will next discuss some principles that we feel should provide the basis for an effective course in secondary English teaching methods.

Criteria for Evaluating Syllabi

A Methods Course Should Be Theoretically Informed

One overriding consideration in course preparation, we feel, is that a course should be *theoretically informed.* In chapter 4 we review the major theories that are stated or implied in the texts read by students in their methods courses. The theories often derive from different psychological principles, such as taking a Piagetian perspective on biological (often referred to as "natural") stages of development or taking a sociocultural perspective on the shaping influence of the environment on thinking. Some courses used texts articulating theoretical perspectives on teaching and learning that emerge from different assumptions about the origins of psychological development (the isolated mind's natural course or the shaping force of the social and cultural environment—the "nature vs. nurture" debate). Some courses juxtaposed incongruous approaches to teaching; they might use as the major text Atwell's *In the Middle,* which presents a student-initiated approach with the teacher playing the role of learner, and also require preservice teachers to design instructional units based on Madeline Hunter's approach, in which the teacher specifies objectives and directs learning. In some syllabi (often reflective courses) we could infer, or even see in the assessments, that the instructor was providing alternative views of teaching in order to give students a range of choices from which to make informed decisions based on their own dispositions as teachers. In others, it appeared that conflicting approaches were being presented without attention to the differences in their theoretical underpinnings.

We feel that students need to be aware of the theories that motivate the teaching approaches they are learning. Some texts used in the courses were stronger theoretically than others. Many claimed to be operating from a theoretical basis, yet rarely revealed what that basis was; these texts tended to be heavy on practical teaching suggestions, such as Tchudi and Tchudi's *The English/Language Arts Handbook* (1991). We believe that regardless of the theory adopted, the texts and teaching approaches that have the best potential for allowing preservice teachers to make informed decisions are those that articulate a theoretical basis for practical activities.

We believe that instructors should make the courses theoretically strong so that students emerge from the methods class with an understanding of how students learn, rather than emerging with a bag of tricks to use. "Trick bag" approaches seem thin in that they give little account of why, when, or whether a teacher should use a particular instructional procedure. Teachers should know the theories that motivate their practice in order to make informed decisions about how to organize their classes and plan instruction for particular groups of students. As would be expected, courses identified as "theoretical" tended to have a strong theoretical basis, though they often gave less attention to the practical application of the theories; workshops and reflective courses were often theoretically driven, with experience-based courses varying in the degree to which they tied theory to practice. Survey courses, we found, tended to have quite a diffuse focus; often, the degree to which they were theoretically informed depended on the extent to which the textbook they relied on articulated a motivating theory.

Learning Should Be Situated in Meaningful Activity

Methods courses should also attend to the need for *situated learning* (Brown, Collins, & Duguid, 1989). Situated learning refers to the relationship between school learning and its potential use in meaningful activity. The knowledge students get in school should serve as a tool for use in their practical work in the world. The value of situated learning seems especially important in a teaching methods class, where the purpose of the course is to prepare students for a very specific kind of professional work.

The syllabi show a number of ways in which the knowledge from the methods course can be situated in meaningful activity. Experience-based courses, for instance, deliberately tie instruction from textbooks and classrooms to field observations, mentoring relationships with practicing teachers, actual teaching and tutoring situations, and other work that makes a direct application of course learning to professional life. Workshop courses often would require students to prepare instructional units that they would eventually use in their student teaching—thus investing their attention to unit design with a pragmatic purpose. Reflective courses would require preservice teachers to consider their own learning experiences in and out of school to discover ways to make school learning more immediate and useful for their own students. The particular ways in which instructors encouraged students to situate their experiences in practical activity varied a great deal, but it seemed to us that those courses that connected knowledge from the course with application to professional life in meaningful and pragmatic ways were of potentially greater help to them in adjusting to life in the classroom.

Learning Should Be Transactional

Another feature of effective teaching and learning is a recognition of the *transactional* nature of communication and learning, a concept that we review when discussing transactional theories of response to literature in chapter 4. Rosenblatt (1978) tries "to counteract the dualistic phrasing of phenomena as an 'interaction' between different factors, because it implies separate, self-contained, and already defined entities acting on one another" (p. 17). She says that "transaction designates, then, an ongoing process in which the elements or factors are, one might say, aspects of a total situation, each conditioned by and conditioning the other" (p. 17). Rosenblatt drew heavily on Dewey, who believed in the value of *activity* in learning. Students should be involved in learning processes, ideally in a manner that engages them with other learners. Social transactions, as characterized by Vygotsky (1978; 1986) and others, are critical to the internalization of new concepts.

As we will review in chapter 3, methods classes provided frequent opportunities for collaboration. In field observations, students often worked in pairs to observe and discuss teaching and learning. In workshop classes, students would often engage in collaborative planning of lessons, using class time to work together on projects over extended periods of time. The classes appeared highly transactional with specific attention paid to involving students in the kinds of processes that they were learning to use in their own teaching. The active approach to learning in such classes, scaffolded by transactions with instructor and peers, is likely to help lead students to the highest levels of potential in their "zone of proximal development," Vygotsky's (1978; 1986) term for the range of potential each person has for learning. The highest range of that zone, he argues, is achieved through transactions with and help from teachers and more capable peers that enable the learner to appropriate new knowledge and grow into more complex understandings.

Often, the degree to which students and teacher engaged in transactional relationships was not apparent through the syllabus. After reading through the syllabi that we present in appendix A, one of the external reviewers of this book wrote that "it was interesting reading these syllabi and the detail with which they outline a semester's work—made me feel guilty about my half-page handouts—still I wonder what happened to negotiating the curriculum." Some methods course teachers do not prepare detailed syllabi, but rather respond to the needs of the students as the course develops. Our conversation with one methods course teacher revealed that he developed a syllabus several weeks into the course after he and the students had discussed what they wanted to focus on, how the class should be conducted, and which texts they should read. The syllabus itself never revealed the manner in which the course content and procedures had been negotiated. Approaches that engage students in the development of the course represent a potentially valuable type of learning transaction, as long as the students have sufficient preparation to contribute constructively to the planning.

Learning Should Be Process-Oriented

Another hallmark of an effective methods class is that it should be *process-oriented*. We hesitate to use this term because it has been applied to virtually every approach imaginable to teaching and therefore has become too diffuse in meaning to have a clear referent. Our own view of process-oriented instruction is that it stresses the long-term and ongoing nature of learning, including the need to allow for play, experimentation, risk, and error in the process of learning new concepts, and also stresses the recursive nature of learning. This view has consequences for teaching and learning, for it underscores the need to allow for extended opportunities to practice, reconsider, revisit, revise, and develop complex ideas, preferably with the help of transactions with other learners and with experts such as instructors and practicing teachers.

We found that workshops were especially likely to allow for this type of learning in that they would cover a large concept such as an instructional unit over a period of many weeks, allowing students to work in class on planning, continue working outside class, return to class for feedback and further development, integrate different parts of the unit at appropriate points, and otherwise work diligently to learn the complex, often messy task of long-term planning. Unit planning, of course, was not the only type of extended, recursive project with potential for process-oriented learning; as we will review in chapter 3, students in many types of classes also kept portfolios of their work, engaged in personal writing that they developed over time, and otherwise pursued projects at length. Our point is that courses which had a specific focus—but which stressed the processes involved in learning that focus—seemed to model the types of learning advocated in the textbooks read much better than did survey courses, which tended to move from one topic to the next with little continuity or extended learning. Following the view of the architect Mies Van Der Rohe, we would argue that "less is more" when choosing the focus for what to accomplish in a teaching methods class.

Students Should Be Involved in Reflection

Related to the last two criteria is the need for *reflection*, the need to make informed choices about assumptions regarding teaching and learning. We wish to introduce another word of caution here about our use of the term "reflection," which we feel has come to mean many things to many people. As we will review in chapter 3, the syllabi provided an abundance of ways in which students can engage in reflection. Often, the journal is evoked as the primary way in which people reflect; on most syllabi, reflection comes about through some sort of assigned writing. We feel, however, that reflection is not necessarily carried out *only* through writing. Both authors of this report consider ourselves to be highly reflective people, yet neither keeps a journal—one of us takes a daily 45-minute walk, during which he reflects on his morning's work; the other spends hours driving around the Oklahoma countryside to supervise student teachers, which provides a soothing opportunity for extended thought.

Our point is that we see reflection coming about in many possible ways, not all of which need to be formal (considering a journal as a formal means of writing) or even in writing. We see, for instance, a great deal of reflection going on when students reconsider their lesson planning in small-group workshop sessions. We see it too when they observe classrooms with a partner and discuss what they have seen. We suspect that students are thoughtful and reflect on their teaching and learning as they walk or drive to and from class, as they fold laundry, or as they engage in other mundane activities. Our purpose with these observations is not to discourage reflective writing, but to point out that other activities encourage reflective thinking as well. By structuring into the methods course other types of activities such as ongoing small-group lesson planning, instructors will further encourage reflection on the part of their students in ways that involve them in thoughtful and considerate activities beyond the conventional written ones.

Learning Should Be Holistic

All of the criteria we have reviewed suggest an umbrella tenet, that learning in the methods class should be *holistic,* another term we use with reservations due to its endless associations. By "holistic" we mean that learning should be continuous and connected, proceeding from whole to parts. The sense of connection must be deliberate; students must see how planning a grammar lesson emerges from a theoretical perspective, responds to sociocultural issues involved in multi-ethnic classrooms, fits in with a larger plan for teaching writing, is connected to other uses of language such as formal and informal discourse, and otherwise is part of a teaching and learning continuum that each instructional moment must fit coherently within.

Survey courses, as we noted previously, tend to present students with an abundance of parts and assume that the students can get a sense of the whole of teaching from them. As we have argued, we believe that limiting the goals of a methods course will result in a better focused, more coherent, and therefore more holistic understanding of teaching.

With a specific focus, a course can accomplish its primary goals, with related secondary goals being subsumed in the larger purpose. Not only will preservice teachers benefit from understanding the linkages among concepts inherent to a holistic approach, their instruction in their own secondary classes ideally will take on the same character, involving them in work that is focused, process-oriented, and accomplished with the big picture in mind.

Students Should Be Involved in Good Work

Our final criterion for evaluating syllabi comes from our belief in the value of *work*. Our notion of work does not conjure the grim and dutiful labor of the Puritan but rather the labor of love of good teachers. We feel that successful teachers are those who work to learn about their profession and continue to work to grow in their teaching. A methods course should be demanding, and by this we mean that it should push students to their highest levels of potential as learners.

By work we *do not* mean that students should do a lot of homework and complete many assignments. Rather, we argue that a well-planned course will put students in what Csikszentmihalyi (1982) has described as the "flow" of an activity, that is, when their motivation and affect are high and when the level of challenge is commensurate with or slightly ahead of their level of ability. When one is "in the flow," time passes quickly as one gets lost in the process of the activity, as often happens when a person is playing a sport at a level of competition that forces utmost concentration, effort, and the greatest execution of skills. Csikszentmihalyi found that the greatest potential for human growth comes when people are involved in activities that place them "in the flow."

We feel that a course in secondary English methods should involve students in good work, work that they find interesting, challenging, and worthwhile, work that pushes their limits and makes time fly by. Our notion of work does not preclude the necessity of play, for teaching—and learning about teaching—should be fun, as it has always been for us. Our criterion of work as a requisite part of a methods course refers to the process that leads to growth and complexity in understanding, infused with high levels of affect and engagement.

To engage students in good work, methods classes should strive to involve the students in activities that are compelling yet challenging, requiring them to draw on a great many resources to learn about the profession of teaching. Demanding projects such as extended units of instruction can push students to synthesize knowledge from many areas into a single, practical project of great personal importance. Central to the completion of such projects is the desire to do a goodly amount of work, a quality we feel is characteristic of successful teachers.

Final Considerations

If we bring all of these criteria to bear on the types of courses we have identified, we conclude that surveys have the least potential for helping to prepare preservice teachers for professional life. All other approaches have different strengths that would provide good experiences to facilitate the transition between preservice and practicing teacher. Surveys, as noted, tended to isolate issues and concepts in single sessions, moving from one topic to the next without returning for further consideration. Surveys rarely gave evidence of collaborative activities or involvement in the processes of learning experienced by secondary students. Often, the students were evaluated according to a great many short assignments, rather than a comprehensive project that they worked on over time which integrated knowledge from many different areas. Ironically, though, the survey was among the most frequently identified means of organization found in the syllabi, a problem that we hope this report will help to change.

As noted, we see many advantages to each of the other approaches. We should point out again that our classification of a syllabus did not preclude it from having attributes found in the other approaches; frequently, workshop courses were theoretically motivated, required journals and other reflective writing, and involved students in field observations as well. In fact, one recommendation that we would make from our review is that a "best" methods course involves elements of workshop, experience-based, theoretical, and reflective courses. While a course will probably have a primary orientation, the qualities of each approach lend themselves to application in any type of course. If we would make any general recommendation from our analysis, it would be for English educators to examine what is exemplary from the various approaches we have identified and to incorporate the qualities they see into their own methods classes.

Our purpose has been to describe the basic approaches to teaching the methods class. We have provided our own criteria for making judgments about the value of different approaches and urge English educators to consider our perspective and develop their own. Just as we wish for preservice teachers to make informed choices about the methods they use in their teaching, we urge those who prepare preservice teachers to understand the possibilities open to them and to design their courses to meet the needs of themselves, their students, and their institutions.

Our review of approaches to teaching the methods class gives a general idea of how the courses are focused. In chapter 3, we take a closer look at the range of assessments and activities engaged in by students, with specific examples from syllabi showing how different courses engaged students in the processes of learning about teaching.

3 Activities and Assessments

METHODS OF EVALUATION

Evaluations of student performance fell into twelve general categories, in the following order of frequency: situated tasks, reflective/personal expression, short planning/teaching assignments, comprehensive projects, reports/critiques of outside reading, medium-length projects, unspecified-length units, literature-related assignments, short tests, long-term planning, analysis of the methods class itself, and classroom management. Our purpose in presenting the following types of assessments is to illustrate ways in which students were evaluated in their methods classes, rather than to contrast the frequency with which each assessment was used. Following is an account of each type of evaluation appearing in each category, with occasional illustrations from the syllabi of forms of evaluation we found representative or exemplary.

Situated Tasks

Seventy-two of the seventy-nine syllabi evaluated students according to their performance in areas that directly tied their coursework to field experiences, teaching demonstrations, professional experiences, and an assortment of efforts to situate coursework in some sort of experiential world. The world of experience was at times observed, at times participated in, at times simulated, and at times integrated into course readings. Twenty-five syllabi included some field-experience component, although the field experiences were not always central activities or assessments in the course. Nine of the syllabi directly tied the course to state department of education documents, learner outcomes, or assessment vehicles, though at times the syllabi did not reveal how those connections were manifested in the course assessments. The effort to evaluate students through their experience in real or simulated teaching situations seems consistent with the NCTE guidelines, which encourage increased involvement in practical field-based activities. Situated tasks fell into the following general areas.

Teaching Demonstrations

One frequent form of situated assessment was for students to demonstrate lessons they had designed for their classmates. Such demonstrations were occasionally videotaped and often were followed by some sort of critique by their classmates.

Working Directly with Students

In some classes, the preservice teachers were required to work directly with either high school or college students. Some syllabi required a tutoring component in a college writing center; others required specific forms of classroom observation such as conducting case studies of secondary students or keeping observation logs of whole classrooms. On occasion, students would be required to teach the classes they observed or grade the papers of the students. One syllabus required students to write an essay contrasting the world of the classroom as represented in their course readings with that which they observed in the classrooms during their field experience.

Joining Professional Organizations

Eight of the syllabi required students to join NCTE and/or the state affiliate, and seven required students to attend a local educational conference, typically the NCTE affiliate conference in the area. A number of other syllabi recommended joining NCTE and requesting book catalogues from educational publishers.

Tying Instruction to State Requirements

Several syllabi made explicit references to state department documents, state assessment programs, state curriculum models, and other special considerations specific to the states in which the students would teach. In addition to being assigned to read such documents and occasionally being tested on them, in some courses preservice teachers were required to prepare instruction that would help their students pass state-mandated tests. One California university, for instance, required students to "choose a work of literature commonly taught at the grade level for which you have signed up, and develop CAP [California Achievement Program] writing prompts designed to lead students INTO, THROUGH, and BEYOND the work. A sample will be distributed."

Simulating Professional Situations

On some syllabi students were required to anticipate future professional needs and activities by filling out job applications, writing letters to prospective department chairs, preparing substitute teacher packets, and creating spreadsheets. Another simulated activity was to analyze "cases" of classroom problems from a course textbook, Small and Strzepek's *A Casebook for English Teachers* (1988).

Analyze Professional Materials

Students in some classes analyzed documents and texts that they would be required to implement in their subsequent teaching. They were at times tested on state department of education documents and manuals, and were required to evaluate the textbooks adopted by their states and the curriculum bulletins from local schools.

Situating Instruction in Hypothetical Settings

Syllabi would often instruct students to imagine a context in which they would teach their lessons and units. One syllabus, for instance, told students that prior to designing their instructional unit, they should

> Create and describe a mythical or real setting in which your teaching will occur. Do this in some detail. By "setting," I mean the community which the school serves and the type of class you are proposing to teach. (Make sure it's an English class, grades 7–12).

Situating instruction in a hypothetical setting would presumably help students consider the contextual factors involved in teaching, such as the way certain books and activities might be received in particular communities, the sociocultural factors affecting the ways in which students learn, the size of the school and classroom, the restrictions of curriculum, and other constraining factors.

Classroom Research

Students making field observations were at times required to conduct a study, often a case study of a particular student, in order to formalize and focus their observation methods. One syllabus required students to

> Focus your observation on one student and try to observe everything that student does for the entire period. Be sure to select someone you can see clearly. In your write-up, try to describe what you could observe of this student's writing process. How much control does the student appear to have and how is this related to the structure of the class? What conclusions do you come to about this student's involvement with the class?

Other syllabi required a more intensive study, with repeated observations of the student, perhaps coupled with interviews and analysis of the student's writing.

Similarly, students might be required to study a student they were tutoring. One syllabus informed students that

> You will be required to tutor a student at the high school or college level in writing for at least one hour per week this semester. I will try to provide volunteers from my entry-level classes, but the ultimate responsibility for finding a tutee is yours.
>
> Tutoring journal: You are responsible for turning in a tutoring journal every week. After each tutoring session, you should write about your impressions of the session—what happened and what you think and feel about it. I will also ask you to include specific things in your journal, such as your assessment of your tutee's writing problems. These journals may be handwritten (but in pen and legible, please)—I expect at least 2–3 pages per week. You should save these journals, as they will form part of the database for your case study.

In this case the journal served not just as a forum for thinking about the student, but as the database for a research project.

Reflective/Personal Expression

The syllabi reinforce the belief that personal reflection is an important part of learning, with fifty-seven of the seventy-nine syllabi requiring what we regard as reflective expression. Reflection was usually encouraged through some sort of writing which, in turn, would be subject to reflection and rethinking. Reflective writing was inevitably a component of reflective courses but often was required in other approaches. Reflective writing appeared in two general areas.

Keeping Logs/Journals

The most frequent mode of reflection was some type of journal or learning log in which students responded to the reading assignments, the class sessions, their field observations, and other course responsibilities. Some courses required specific types of journals, such as dialogue journals, to be shared with either a class partner or the teacher. The journals served as ways for students to think about and synthesize the various experiences they were having with the course. Some courses required that journals be turned in periodically during the semester; others required a single journal turned in at the end, often as part of a portfolio. Most courses allowed the contents of the journals to be open-ended, though a few specified that "correct grammar and usage" were required.

In reflective courses, the log often counted as a great portion of the student's grade. As one syllabus told the students,

Because of the nature of this class and the emphasis on the reader-response theory of literature study, the response logs will constitute a major portion of the grade. Emphasis on the logs is not accidental; logs are considered to be a major emphasis of the course.

Some logs were "dialogue journals" that the instructor or other students would respond to. One syllabus described the students' responsibility in the following way:

The journal will be used in class as a way of establishing dialogue. Often, we will exchange journals for fifteen minutes of class time and write responses to one another's entries—in the manner of a written conversation. This will enable us to focus the oral discussion, and should also foster the interactive atmosphere which is so conducive to learning. NOTE: Please leave room in your notebook for response comments, either by double spacing or by using only one side of the paper. I keep a reading journal also, and will participate in these exchanges.

The larger purpose for response journals is simply to enable readers the opportunity to think in writing about textual material. I will collect journals twice during the semester . . . for response and evaluation. Students may use their journals during the final exam.

As this instructor informs the students, their reflections should provide the beginnings of larger dialogues and discussions about the course readings.

Directed Reflection

In addition, students were required to engage in more directed reflection through assignments such as writing a literacy autobiography, developing a personal teaching philosophy, writing about a favorite teacher, and otherwise thinking about the experiences that had shaped their own reading and writing development in order to get them to understand their own values and orientation. Students were then encouraged to share these reflections with other students to get a sense of the range of experience that diverse groups of students bring to a single classroom. Presumably, such sharing and reflection would help make the preservice teachers more aware of and sensitive to the backgrounds of the students they would eventually teach.

Engagement in reflective writing often provided an opportunity for students to participate in the processes they were being encouraged to use with their students. Typically, students would be given class time to respond to one another's reflective writing in peer-response groups and then be given opportunities for revision or further writing. Reflective writing, then, seemed designed to serve two purposes: to encourage reflection on the part of the preservice teachers themselves as they experienced the course and to help give them procedures for running their own classes.

The following directed reflection is a "reading autobiography" and represents the type of assignment often found on syllabi:

> Students should write a short (approximately 5–6 double-spaced pages) history of their literacy for presentation in class. Each should consider the events and circumstances of learning to read. What are the earliest memories of reading? What specific books do you recall? What *words* do you remember learning to read? What pleasures and/or problems do you associate with early memories of reading? What about phonics? How did your reading habits change when you went to school—and later, over the twelve years of your education? And so on.
>
> This is an informal paper, but should be polished so as to represent your abilities as a soon-to-be English teacher. Your audience is your classmates who, like you, are trying to understand how and why people read and what this means for classroom instruction.

The instructor went on to request permission to use the students' essays for research purposes, which would appear to contribute to the importance of the project and acquaint the students with the instructor's research interests. The idea of using student reflections for the instructor's research purposes was not common, however. The purpose appeared to be to help preservice teachers see ways in which they could undertake their own classroom investigations and begin to see the importance of teacher research.

Reflection on Teaching

A few syllabi required students to write reflections on instructional ideas they had developed. On one syllabus, for instance, students were required to

> Select three correlative writing/grammar concepts you feel students need to learn to become better writers. Then, in a two-page paper, show the step-by-step procedure you will follow in leading your students to a clear understanding of your three concepts, i.e., what kinds of activities, assignments (homework). Discussions will be necessary to teach the three concepts to the grade level (7–12) and ability level for which this plan is being designed. In a short paragraph heading up this plan, state your three correlative concepts and answer the following questions:

   a. Why am I teaching these three concepts?
   b. Why will my students write better compositions as a result of this lesson (or series of lessons)?
   c. Describe two writing assignments to test whether or not you have connected with the students and tell how you will evaluate (grade) these two assignments.

In this sort of assignment the students are asked to reflect on the ways in which their teaching will affect their students, rather than on their own personal experiences.

Short Planning/Teaching Assignments

Students were frequently required to produce short assignments such as the lessons that either stand alone or make up the parts of larger teaching units, with fifty-five of the seventy-nine syllabi including assessment of short planning/teaching assignments. Typically, students would plan some sort of grammar lesson, "mini-lesson," or a smaller component of what presumably would fit into a larger instructional sequence. On four syllabi, students were required to situate their lesson planning in their student teaching by planning their lessons under the supervision of their cooperating teachers. We identified five general types of short assignments on the syllabi.

Lessons

Often, students were required to produce a series of lessons, perhaps one for grammar, one for composition, and one for literature. The lessons appeared to last a single class period or less, in that they were often used as teaching demonstrations during methods course classes. Syllabi usually did not spell out the specifics for the assignments, relying instead on the textbook or supplemental handouts for details of what should be involved.

Simulated Student Behavior

Some syllabi required students to engage in the processes involved in particular types of assignments. One routinely required students to respond to prompts that they might in turn use with students, such as "In your journal, describe a place or narrate an event with which you are familiar that relates to a theme or themes in "Prufrock.' Let us see the place or event in such a way that we can begin to understand its relationship to the theme." The writing they did in response to these prompts both served to engage them in the processes involved in such writing and also was turned in to the instructor for a grade.

Mini-Lessons

Many classes required students to teach "mini-lessons" modeled on the procedures described by Atwell (1987). A mini-lesson is a brief (roughly five-minute) introduction to a writing or reading problem or skill, such as finding a way to initiate a personal narrative. Kirby, Liner, and Vinz's *Inside/Out* (1988) often served as a good reference for quick assignments that get students immediately into their writing.

Subparts of Lessons and Units

Lessons were further broken down into components such as objectives, test questions, prereading activities, and discussion-leading questions which were turned in for evaluation. Although these assignments were treated separately and usually graded, they would also often contribute toward the construction of a longer lesson.

Collections of Smaller Assignments

Some syllabi required what were variously known as activity cards, activity packets, resource boxes, and learning files. These were collections of smaller assignments, a form of portfolio for practical teaching ideas. Several syllabi referred students to Tchudi and Tchudi's *The English/Language Arts Handbook* (1991) for instructions on how to prepare activity cards (pp. 44–47):

> We do these on eight-and-a-half-by-eleven-inch pieces of poster board, with glued on graphics, instructions, photographs. In simpler form, activity cards can be some instructions typed or handwritten on an index card.
>
> Each activity card contains a task or assignment, plus instructions on how to complete it. You can construct activity cards for:
>
> Writing assignments.
>
> Study questions for literary works.
>
> Individual projects done in conjunction with thematic teaching.
>
> Individualized reading.
>
> Whether or not you have a permanent classroom, you might construct sets of cards for particular units you're teaching. At appropriate points, open up your box of cards and allow students to select the ones on which they want to work. You'll achieve instant individualization (backed up with a good deal of preparation).

Collections of smaller assignments, then, provided preservice teachers with an abundance of short assignments they could have on file.

Comprehensive Projects

A comprehensive project was a large undertaking that typically involved a synthesis of learning over a long period of time and was included on fifty syllabi. Midterm and final exams, portfolios, and long instructional units were the general types of comprehensive projects found on the syllabi.

Midterm and Final Exams

We included midterm and final exams in this category, even though the content of such exams was rarely specified in the syllabi. In most cases we were unable to infer the content of the exams, and therefore could not tell what types of thinking students were engaged in throughout the experience of the exam. We would hope that a good comprehensive exam would engage students in the sorts of reflective and analytic thinking that the courses purported to be emphasizing and that appeared to be an important part of the other comprehensive forms of evaluation. Syllabi were much more careful about spelling out the requirements of portfolios and long instructional units.

Portfolios

Portfolios often included a variety of in-process projects the students had worked on during the semester, perhaps including their journals, teaching units, reflective writing, classroom observations, and other writing and/or collected materials through which they had thought through the issues from the course. Some portfolios were miscellaneous collections of the various work from the semester; others required an organizational structure. Some syllabi gave suggestions on how to use the portfolio for reflection and learning. One syllabus informed the students that

> We will at times go back to earlier work for revision and similar activities, and keeping such folders will help you experience the benefit of having a writing portfolio. Although the writing we do in class is a means for investigating the nature of writing rather than an end in itself, you will probably find that you want to go back over these writings and save some of them after the course is over.

The portfolio thus enabled students to keep a record of their various writing from the semester, with the prospect of returning to it for further consideration and development, perhaps even after the formal conclusion of the methods class.

We next review three types of ways in which syllabi presented the idea of a portfolio to students. We then discuss ways in which portfolios were assessed.

Portfolios of personal writing. One type of portfolio focused on getting students to consider themselves as writers. They were not required to include any of their formal teaching plans, but rather were required to keep the various drafts of the more personal and reflective essays that they had worked on. One such syllabus required the following:

> A Writing Portfolio containing all in-class writing, assigned writing, and experimental pieces you do on your own (12 pieces), plus all drafts, jottings, notes, and revisions of the pieces you work on for this portfolio. SAVE EVERYTHING!!! The goals of this part of the course are: (a) "Stretching" and experimentation with some of the kinds of writing secondary students might be expected to do; (b) Practice with generating, responding, revising, and editing; (c) Preparation of a portfolio of varied writings, some still in draft form, others revised, and a reflection on your own progress as a writer in this course.

The approach appeared to serve two purposes: to get preservice teachers to become more reflective about their own writing and to help them understand the benefits of such a process approach to writing so that they would be more likely to encourage it with their own students.

Selected pieces, organized according to a theme. Another approach to portfolios was to have the writers present their reflections through an initial statement of purpose, a series of selected papers, and a final statement of direction. In such portfolios students were not demonstrating their own full exploration of the processes that had led them to their final written products, but were selecting those products that best represented their learning from the semester. One syllabus required at the outset of the portfolio "an introduction in which you explain to your reader why you have selected certain items for inclusion and how you have organized your materials." The syllabus went on to specify certain requirements, such as a statement of teaching philosophy, an open-ended essay, a unit plan, and two responses to assignments from the semester, all culled from a larger range of writing produced during the semester. Students were then required to provide "a concluding statement in which you map out the questions you expect to explore as a student-teacher and how you might go about researching those questions." The portfolio, therefore, served not only as a collection of work selected by the students as representative of what they had learned, but also as a framework and catalyst for an inquiry central to their teaching.

Collections of all work from the semester. Some syllabi required a portfolio of everything the student had written during the semester. At times, we questioned whether or not this approach captured the spirit of the portfolio, in that the items within it were often evaluated separately, with a few additional points awarded for their being collected together.

Assessment of portfolios. Criteria for evaluating portfolios varied. Most syllabi identified a percentage of the student's grade that the portfolio would account for, ranging from 5 percent to 80 percent of the semester grade. The syllabus often did not reveal how a portfolio was assessed.

One syllabus did include a set of evaluation criteria, though the specific way in which students would be measured against them wasn't clear. The syllabus included a list of areas that would be evaluated, including organization, learning (broken down into outside reading, additional activities that contribute to learning, and relationship to methods class), philosophical base, and presentation. Each of these areas could receive one of three rankings: strong evidence, some evidence, or little/no evidence of performance. The grading rubric did not specify what constituted "strong evidence" of having any of the properties evaluated, although the instructor may have conveyed that understanding through means not identified on the syllabus.

Longer Instructional Units

Instructional units of three to eight weeks incorporated all of the practical work done throughout the semester in an integrated, usually thematic approach to some aspect of literary study. Long thematic literature units were usually taught according to the principles presented in a course textbook and/or supplemental handouts and were most frequently required in classes using the workshop approach. Workshops typically involved students in in-class planning of lessons and presented material recursively; in other words, students might plan lessons collaboratively in one class, demonstrate them to classmates in another, and revise them collaboratively in another. Workshops tended to stress the connection of different types of instructional planning so that longer units could be conceived and planned over the course of time.

One syllabus devoted the second half of each class session to a unit-planning workshop in which students would work in groups of three to four to plan a comprehensive unit. The workshop portion of the class allowed students to incorporate the particular ideas from the session's reading assignments and class discussions into their larger planning ideas, and to make an immediate connection between a specific idea (such as planning prereading activities) and other aspects of instruction. The units developed during the workshop component could be used by the students as practice for their formal units written outside class or could be turned in for a grade if the groups of students so chose.

Some classes planned their units around literature that the class had read as a whole, with small groups of students planning units. Other units were planned in conjunction with the student's anticipated cooperating teacher. Of these units, some were written under the teacher's supervision, others with the teacher's more direct collaboration.

Some syllabi provided extensive work sheets on how to develop a unit plan; others relied on the textbooks. A number of classes provided opportunities for feedback on the units, both as they were being developed and during final sharing sessions. Some classes required or encouraged students to share their completed units with their classmates, with one syllabus specifying that all units would be bound and available through the neighborhood copy shop.

Reports/Critiques of Outside Reading

Forty syllabi specified that students should engage in outside reading, with the readings coming from reserve or recommended reading lists, suggested professional journals (often the *English Journal*), and occasionally research in English education. Students were then evaluated in some way on their outside reading. The evaluations came in four ways.

Abstracts

Students were often required to read twenty or so journal articles not on the course syllabus and write either an abstract of each or an annotated bibliography of a whole set. The outside reading lists were often from professional journals, typically the *English Journal* or other practitioner-oriented journals and occasionally a research journal.

Reactions to Articles

Students were also required to write more extensive reactions to a smaller set of articles, perhaps five. These reactions took different forms, at times being critical, at other times being evaluative, and at still other times involving summary.

Presentations on Outside Reading

Following their reactions to outside reading, students were at times required to present their findings or responses in an oral presentation to their classmates, sometimes followed by a discussion of the issues involved.

Symposia

A more extensive analysis of topics from outside reading came through symposia presented by small groups of students. They would be given an extended portion of the class time to explore a topic researched outside of class, presumably engaging their classmates in discussion of issues that would affect their teaching.

Medium-Length Projects

Twenty-eight syllabi included projects that involved a medium-length synthesis of ideas encountered in the course. The projects fell primarily into two areas, open-topic papers on issues of interest to the students and two- to three-week instructional units of study that incorporated ideas from the smaller assignments designed for the course.

Medium-Length Papers

The open-topic papers were often theoretical. One syllabus required "three short but more formal papers addressing issues in the teaching of writing, language, and literature." Students might write a five- to ten-page paper on Rosenblatt's transactional theory of the literary work, on cooperative learning, on whole language, or on some other topic that had been stimulated by either their reading for the course or their encounters during field experience.

Short Instructional Units

The instructional units assigned on the syllabi were often of short duration, one or two weeks, and cover a specific topic or area. Students might be required, for instance, to write a one-week composition unit and a one-week grammar unit. On other occasions, a syllabus would require students to provide an overall plan for a long instructional unit with specific lessons provided for one or two weeks.

Unspecified Units

Twenty-seven syllabi required instructional units, but never specified a particular length.

Literature-Related Assignments

Nineteen syllabi required students to read literature as part of the methods class. Often, the literature would serve as a vehicle for group activities in the planning of instruction; at other times, students would read the literature in order to become familiar with the texts they would presumably teach in schools.

Reading Literature for Instructional Planning

At times, the students would be required to read specific works that they would be likely to teach in a secondary English class. Some syllabi included sessions during which small groups of students would plan a way in which to teach the text. Students would then share the lessons and activities they had planned in order to see the different ways in which a novel could be taught. On some occasions, students were required to provide copies of the lessons they had prepared for their classmates. Occasionally, the teaching approach taken by the different groups was subjected to a theoretical analysis, with students attempting to identify the theoretical perspectives from which the different lessons had been planned.

Reports on Literature

Students were also required to read novels on their own and provide either personal reactions to them or reports to their classmates on what the books were about. These reports could be either written, presented orally, or both. The purpose was to familiarize the class with novels (particularly young adult literature) frequently taught in secondary school.

Short Tests

On seven syllabi students were required to take quizzes over assigned readings, and on a few syllabi students were tested on either grammar or state-required knowledge. Tests of this sort appeared to be concerned with reporting correct answers, as opposed to the more constructive nature of most of the rest of the assignments on the syllabi.

Long-Term Planning

Six syllabi required students to sketch out some sort of long-term teaching plan, such as a semester curriculum or grading-period syllabus. Details of such assignments were often limited.

Reflection on/Analysis of the Methods Class Itself

Three syllabi required students to reflect on particular methods class sessions through required writing. Guest speakers and teaching demonstrations were the subjects of reflective or evaluative papers, and one class required a daily log to be kept, with a different student recording each class:

> As practice for making effective classroom observations, each student will take a turn(s) as participant-observer in our own class sessions. This will involve sitting apart from the class and making qualitative notes regarding the class proceedings—recording as many details as possible.

Included in the observations, continued the assignment, might be attention to the time spent on segments of the class, the physical arrangement of the room, the number of participants in discussions, and questions about why particular events had taken place.

Classroom Management

Two syllabi required students to either prepare or critique a plan for effective classroom management, typically drawing on the course readings for information on how to do so.

COLLABORATIVE ACTIVITIES

In addition to the assessments, students engaged in other types of activities. We were particularly interested in the extent to which the methods classes required students to work collaboratively, in that most of the course readings stressed either the social nature of learning or, even in more individualized approaches, advocated dialogue journals, peer evaluation of writing, and other forms of cooperation and collaboration. Presumably, if a course effectively teaches preservice teachers the value of collaborative, cooperative, or small-group learning, then it would need to consciously provide such experiences for the students so that they could appreciate the benefits themselves.

We will next review the types of collaborative learning that we found in the syllabi. We should caution that we do not expect that the frequency of collaboration we found specified on the syllabi accurately represents the extent to which collaboration actually took place in the classes; we find it likely that many classes included small-group activities and other forms of collaboration that were not identified on the syllabi. We offer the following ideas in order to show potential areas in which collaboration can take place in a methods class, rather than to make a judgment on the extent to which we know such collaboration occurs. In general, collaboration fell into two areas: collaboration during learning and collaboration as a form of response or feedback.

Collaboration during Learning

The first type of collaboration, we found, concerned collaboration during the process of learning something new. The purpose of the collaboration appeared to be to serve as an instructional scaffold, providing peer support for the learning of a new concept. We found that the collaborative activities that took place to support learning-in-process fell into the following areas: the overall structure of the class, the overall ethos of the class, the analysis of issues, the planning of instruction, the analysis of teaching, and participation in learning experiences. We will next review examples of each type of collaborative activity we found in the syllabi.

The Overall Structure of the Class

Some syllabi stated directly to the students that the overall structure of the class would involve collaborative learning. One syllabus informed students that the course would have a "seminar format" that required their participation and input; others stressed to students the need for their participation in the class in order for them to have a fruitful experience. As reviewed previously, another syllabus devoted half of every session to a "workshop" in which small groups of students developed instructional units upon which their independent units would be based. In such classes, cooperation was a fundamental part of the overall classroom structure.

The Overall Ethos of the Class

One syllabus included a message to the students that stressed the cooperative nature of the class:

> This course is absolutely noncompetitive. I hope you all get A's. There is no reason we shouldn't work together; in fact, on any of the assignments, should you decide to collaborate with

another person, that's fine with me. That's especially true for the final project. Let me know of your plans and I'll give you some tips on collaboration.

This syllabus reflects my thinking before the academic year. The content is negotiable. This syllabus is only a plan, but I do not yet have specific students and specific needs in mind, and that could make a big difference. We'll talk.

With this message, the instructor has established an ethos of co-operation among the students, encouraging them to support one another in their learning. Other syllabi that we examined included elements of this message, such as encouraging students to collaborate on their major projects and letting students know that the course requirements were flexible. We imagine that students in such a class would indeed be moved to look upon learning as a cooperative experience and eventually encourage their own students to work collaboratively with their peers.

The Analysis of Issues

Often, students would work in small groups to analyze issues covered in the course. Students might, for instance, conduct panel discussions on outside reading related to issues covered in the course. They might attend professional conferences in groups and report their experiences to the class. Some classes included small-group or roundtable discussions of professional issues that were suggested by the course readings; at times, small groups of students led the whole class in the exploration of an issue or problem. One class began each session with "Explorations and Inquiries," a twenty-minute period in which small groups discussed the week's reading assignment, followed by a whole-class discussion of the groups' responses.

The Planning of Instruction

Students were often required to work in small groups to plan instruction. As noted, some classes allowed students to collaborate on all projects completed in the course, including their major instructional units. Frequently, class time was devoted to small-group planning of lessons and units, most often in workshops.

The Analysis of Teaching

Students would work in groups to analyze actual teaching and students. In their field observations, students were at times required to visit classes in pairs or groups, presumably so that they could share their observations. Some students were required to form teacher-researcher groups so that when they made their field observations, they could have a common ground for analyzing and discussing the teaching they observed. Others were required to do team teaching for the practicum that accompanied the methods course.

Participation in Learning Experiences

A final way in which students collaborated during learning was when they participated in the types of experiences discussed in their textbooks. One syllabus required students to participate in a "writing workshop," which appeared to involve them in the sorts of peer response inherent in the workshop setting. Other syllabi, as noted previously, involved students in the type of small-group peer feedback that they were being encouraged to use in their own teaching. On the one hand, this form of collaboration represented response or feedback, which we discuss next; on the other, it served as a learning experience itself, in that it engaged the students in the process of sharing writing.

Collaboration as a Form of Response or Feedback

In addition to allowing for collaboration during a learning process, many courses instituted opportunities for peer feedback and sharing of in-process or finished writing or projects, or for assessing one another's teaching. We found that this collaborative response fell into three general areas: response to personal writing, response to instructional design, and the evaluation of teaching and materials. We will next review each of these three areas.

Response to Personal Writing

Some syllabi required students to engage in the sorts of personal writing advocated by the textbooks they read for the course. Often, such classes were categorized as having a "reflective" orientation. Students typically engaged in the same processes suggested by the textbooks, including having students meet in small groups for feedback, response, support, and criticism. At times, the collaboration came through dialogue journals which the students would exchange with regular partners and at times with the instructor.

Response to Instructional Design

Many classes included opportunities for feedback from other students on lessons and units that students were developing; this happened most frequently in workshops. Often, the feedback came after a first effort, with students then given further opportunities to use the response to improve their instruction. This type of response seemed most helpful when students were engaged in long planning processes such as the integration of a series of lessons into a larger instructional unit; students could receive extensive and continuous feedback from peers on ideas that they were developing over a period of time, thus making it likely for them to see the connections among the different parts of the unit they were developing.

The Evaluation of Teaching and Materials

Students were often assigned to work in groups to evaluate something they had read or observed. Many classes required students to demonstrate lessons they had designed, and then had them provide constructive feedback for one another. Small groups of students would also discuss textbooks that had been adopted by the states in which they would teach, sharing their appraisals with the class.

Discussion of Assessments and Activities

Our review of the forms of assessments and activities describes a vast array of ways in which students are evaluated in undergraduate secondary English methods classes. Our goal at this point is not to identify the "best" ways to assess students, but to present a world of possibilities for teacher-educators to consider. The "best" means of assessment in a methods class is undoubtedly tied to the context of instruction and the ways in which the course is organized.

Some types of assessment seem well suited to (or at least more frequently used in) particular types of course organization. Survey courses tended to rely on short assignments and tests and on midterm and final exams, with instructional units of often unspecified length; surveys rarely showed any opportunities for collaborative learning. Workshop courses typically involved a great deal of collaboration and required a comprehensive project such as a long instructional unit that was developed, critiqued, and revised over a period of many weeks. Experience-based courses situated assessment in field observations and activities, often with reflection in logs. Reflective courses frequently relied on reflective types of writing for assessment, including logs and accounts of personal experiences as learners, with the work often submitted in a portfolio. Theoretical courses often required medium-length projects such as a series of ten-page papers on professional issues and exams requiring long essays.

These tendencies, of course, mask the unique ways in which each syllabus accounted for assessment. Different instructors mixed evaluations according to their own situations, resulting in a dual focus in several cases and, in most cases, calling on a principled mix of the various methods we have described. If we were to make one general recommendation to those who teach the methods course, it would be to consider all the possibilities revealed through the assessments we have described and to look for ways to incorporate those which they find most compelling into their own courses.

Following the criteria we laid out at the end of chapter 2, we would urge English educators to situate assessment and activities in meaningful professional activities, encourage reflection in some way, evaluate students in ways that enable them to integrate knowledge through a synthesis of the course material, and involve students in challenging, engaging, and transforming experiences. We feel that the potential for helping students to grow into more complex thinkers, more theoretically grounded teachers, more motivated professionals, more reflective human beings, and more inquiring teachers is available through many of the activities and assignments we have characterized in this chapter. The types of assessments used by individual teacher-educators in their methods courses should come from their analysis of their own teaching situations and judgment about what will most benefit their students.

The activities and assessments used in methods classes were often closely related to the texts that students were required to read. In chapter 4, we analyze the books that appeared on the syllabi. Through our reading of these texts, we found that they represented several different theoretical perspectives on teaching and learning. In chapter 4, we discuss the major theoretical perspectives that students are being exposed to in the methods class and review the texts through which those perspectives are articulated.

4 Theories and Issues Represented in Syllabi

In this chapter we review the different theoretical positions and issues that are assumed or articulated by the texts students were assigned to read on the syllabi. Typically, the beliefs about learning that underlie the texts are presented straightforwardly to students, often dismissing other theories in the process. Some texts rely on research findings to justify their theoretical orientations; others rely on introspection by the authors; still others rely on experience regarding "what works" in real classrooms. From a study based solely on the syllabi, we have no idea of the extent to which preservice teachers accept the theories being presented. We can assume, however, that the theories to which they are initially exposed—especially if they are the exclusive theories presented to them in their teaching methods course—are likely to influence their teaching to some extent, at least at the outset of their careers.

The review of each perspective delineated in this chapter includes (1) the label we have given to a theory or issue; (2) the texts listed on the syllabi which subscribe to that position or are concerned with that issue; and (3) a review of what the position entails and how it is treated in a sample from the texts. The reviews of the positions are not comprehensive, in that each text is not necessarily summarized or included in the discussion. We have made an effort to discuss the most frequently used texts, and on some occasions have included references to less-often used texts that illustrate some point particularly well. The placement of a particular text in a particular category is to some degree subjective, and without question, several of the texts could easily be cross-referenced to other categories.

In making the following classifications, we recall the words of Britton, Burgess, Martin, McLeod, and Rosen (1975): "We classify at our peril. Experiments have shown that even the lightest touch of the classifier's hand is likely to induce us to see members of a class as more alike than they actually are, and items from different classes as less alike than they actually are" (p. 1). We have tried to place each text under the category where it seems most appropriate in terms of the position with which we find it primarily concerned, with the understanding that most texts are multifaceted and include discussions of many issues.

This problematic aspect of categorizing the texts is particularly true of some of the comprehensive textbooks that are used as the basic text in many classes. Although these textbooks are intended to survey the field, we have found nonetheless that some do so from a particular perspective. Covering a lot of ground does not necessarily require a book to be theoretically eclectic. Our judgment regarding a placement is intended to help readers identify the perspective from which the authors view the field.

In writing the following characterizations of positions, we have made an effort to represent the perspectives through the words of the authors and to avoid making judgments about their validity. At times, the effort was great because several of the perspectives rely on sharply contrasting assumptions about human development, social relations, and the respective roles of students and teachers in classrooms. As will become apparent at some points, one of the authors of this study has contributed to a perspective that relies on quite different assumptions from one of the others. Nonetheless we have made every effort to represent as fairly as possible positions operating from different assumptions.

We also wish to acknowledge that although we are describing perspectives that are often seemingly at odds with one another, we understand that a great many practicing teachers freely adopt strategies from a variety of texts, whether or not the motivating theories are consistent with one another. We also found that many syllabi required students to read texts that seemed to represent conflicting theoretical perspectives; we can think of several reasons for such a decision, including the need to provide a balanced perspective, the wish to illustrate theoretical contrasts, or perhaps just a personal fondness for certain texts in spite of their different assumptions about teaching and learning. In making distinctions, we are not offering a forced choice. Rather, we are attempting to identify the range of theories available in the texts most often used on methods course syllabi.

The categories that we have developed are not always symmetrical. For instance, two of the categories, "Piagetian Approaches Based on the Assumption of Natural Development" and "Approaches Involving the Concept of Instructional Scaffolding," include texts that cover a range of language arts activities such as response to literature, writing, oral activities, and many other strands of the curriculum. "Transactional Theories of Literary Response," on the other hand, primarily concerns the teaching and learning of literature; "Language as Process" concerns ways of learning grammar and other aspects of linguistic structure; and "Sociocultural Perspectives on Learning" is less about teaching methods and more about understanding students' backgrounds. At times, these texts overlap, such as when a text advocates instructional scaffolding in the service of promoting a literary transaction. Again, we have developed these categories to identify the central focus of each text and to review the different theories the texts present to students. As we mentioned earlier, some of the authors whose works we categorize might disagree with our decisions; our own editor requested that we move one of his books from one category to another, and perhaps his co-author might prefer yet a third category. Our goal is not to provide a reductionist classification of texts but to identify the theories most commonly presented and to provide a list of texts that methods course teachers have used to represent those theories.

The following analysis consists of two parts. The first part provides a review of the theories or issues that were represented by a minimum of ten texts on course syllabi; we assume these to be the theories regarding learning and teaching that preservice teachers would most frequently be taught. The second part provides book lists from theories or topics that were also represented on the syllabi, though with less frequency. We include no discussion of these less-frequently covered issues, but rather present the texts that were either required or recommended as references for teacher-educators.

Each section opens with two lists of texts classified under the theoretical approach we have identified, the first list identifying the frequency with which a text was required and then recommended (identified in brackets), the second list identifying books that either were put on reserve or were from short lists of highly recommended texts (with the frequency in brackets). The texts have been gathered from all syllabi submitted to the study, including courses that complemented the methods course, such as classes in teaching writing, young adult literature, and other related topics. Although we did not include an analysis of the syllabi of these complementary courses in chapter 2, we include the texts in this chapter because they are central to the learning about the teaching of English/language arts that students experienced during their preservice teaching programs.

The following sections review the texts and theoretical approaches most frequently represented on methods course syllabi. We address them in the order in which they are most frequently represented in texts, starting with the theory students are exposed to most often.

MAJOR THEORETICAL POSITIONS

Piagetian Approaches Based on the Assumption of Natural Development

Required/Recommended

Atwell, N. (1987). *In the middle: Writing, reading, and learning with adolescents.* Portsmouth, NH: Boynton/Cook-Heinemann. [13/5]

Calkins, L.M. (1986). *The art of teaching writing.* Exeter, NH: Heinemann. [1/2]

Elbow, P. (1973). *Writing without teachers.* New York: Oxford University Press. [1/4]

Elbow, P. (1981). *Writing with power: Techniques for mastering the writing process.* New York: Oxford University Press. [2/3]

Elbow, P. (1986). *Embracing contraries: Explorations in teaching and learning.* New York: Oxford University Press. [1/1]

Goldberg, N. (1986). *Writing down the bones.* Boston: Shambala. [1/0]

Kirby, D., Liner, T., & Vinz, R. (1988). *Inside out: Developmental strategies for teaching writing.* 2nd ed. Portsmouth, NH: Boynton/Cook-Heinemann. [14/7]

Macrorie, K. (1970). *Telling writing.* New York: Hayden. [1/4]

Macrorie, K. (1988). *The I-search paper.* Portsmouth, NH: Boynton/Cook-Heinemann. [1/5]

Moffett, J. (1981). *Coming on center: Essays in English education.* Portsmouth, NH: Boynton/Cook-Heinemann. [1/2]

Moffett, J., & Wagner, B.J. (1992). *A student-centered language arts curriculum, grades 7–12.* 4th ed. Portsmouth, NH: Boynton/Cook-Heinemann. [4/7]

Murray, D.M. (1968). *A writer teaches writing: A practical method of teaching composition.* Boston: Houghton-Mifflin. [4/4]

Murray, D.M. (1984). *Write to learn.* New York: Holt, Rinehart & Winston. [1/1]

Murray, D.M. (1991). *The craft of revision.* New York: Holt, Rinehart & Winston. [1/3]

Newkirk, T. (1986). *To compose: Teaching writing in the high school.* Portsmouth, NH: Boynton/Cook-Heinemann. [2/0]

Proett, J., & Gill, K. (1986). *The writing process in action: A handbook for teachers.* Urbana, IL: National Council of Teachers of English. [4/1]

Romano, T. (1987). *Clearing the way: Working with teenage writers.* Portsmouth, NH: Boynton/Cook-Heinemann. [5/0]

Tchudi, S.N., & Mitchell, D. (1989). *Explorations in the teaching of English.* 3rd ed. New York: HarperCollins. [27/10]

Tchudi, S.N., & Tchudi, S.J. (1991). *The English/language arts handbook: Class-room strategies for teachers.* Rev. ed. Portsmouth, NH: Boynton/Cook-Heinemann. [10/7]

Recommended

Berthoff, A. (1978). *Forming/thinking/writing.* Rochelle Park: Hayden. [4]

Emig, J. (1971). *The composing processes of twelfth graders.* NCTE Research Report No. 13. Urbana, IL: National Council of Teachers of English. [8]

Graves, D. (1983). *Writing: Teachers and children at work.* Portsmouth, NH: Boynton/Cook-Heinemann. [5]

Tchudi, S.N. (1986). *English teachers at work: Ideas and strategies from five countries.* Portsmouth, NH: Boynton/Cook-Heinemann. [3]

The first position that we will review is without question the most widely represented perspective found in the syllabi. Books co-authored by Stephen Tchudi appeared on nearly half of the syllabi, and four of the most widely used texts in the study were categorized under this position (Atwell, 1987; Kirby et al., 1988; Tchudi & Mitchell, 1989; and Tchudi & Tchudi, 1991). With the exception of Atwell, these texts are also among the most venerable books found on the syllabi, with Kirby et al. originally published in 1981, Tchudi and Mitchell in 1974, and Tchudi and Tchudi in 1979.

The epistemological position shared by these texts is that a learner's development is "natural," with the implication that the learner has a pure sense of self that is changed and possibly corrupted when it comes in contact with the outside world, particularly when overly influenced by a teacher's directives. This view of human nature has ancient and widely accepted roots in Western thought, with Rousseau, Freud, and Piaget among its greatest exponents. Due to their belief in students' natural development, the authors recommend that teachers play a facilitating, rather than leading, role in students' progress. Tchudi and Tchudi inform the reader in the preface of their book that "we're committed to a philosophy of English/language arts education that's variously and synonymously labeled *student centered, holistic, whole language, experience centered*, or *personal growth*" (p. vi), perspectives McCarthey and Raphael (1992) associate with Piagetian conceptions of development that attribute development to biological, rather than social, changes and influences (e.g., Piaget, 1977). The following sections review the basic premises of the writers categorized in this section.

Developmental Approach

Authors subscribing to this position argue that a child's natural development should be cultivated in the classroom, with attention paid to the stage of development appropriate to particular levels of schooling. Tchudi and Mitchell argue that a child should not "be treated as a *remedial adult*" (p. 38). Tchudi and Mitchell contrast their approach with "a more traditional approach" (p. 48) in which students are taught skills that they will presumably need later on in life, maintaining that language learning is "naturalistic" (p. 48) and that the "teacher needs to be very cautious about supplying information or giving overt instruction" (p. 51) because direct instruction will disrupt or distort the natural growth of the child.

The title of Kirby et al.'s *Inside Out: Developmental Strategies for Teaching Writing* deliberately suggests two fundamental assumptions regarding development. The first is that writing proceeds from the *inside out*. As the authors say in their opening paragraph,

> It all begins inside; inside the heads of our kids. There are ideas in there and language and lots of possibilities. Writing is a pulling together of that inside stuff. Writing is a rehearsal in meaning making. What we like to call "mind texts." The teacher's role in all this is to support those rehearsals, to help kids bring those mind texts to the page as powerful writings. It's the head-to-page trip that is so frightening and difficult for writers. (p. 1)

The authors adhere to a Cartesian distinction between mind and matter that is often associated with the work of Piaget. Writers' ideas are locked inside their heads, unable to come out; the teacher's task is to create an environment in which the writing, which already exists in the form of ideas, comes out and makes itself public. Murray (1984) similarly argues that, although writers should share their writing with peers, teachers, and others, "in the end, the writer at eighteen or eighty is alone with the writer's own experience and the writer's own language. The writer, in that loneliness, keeps learning to write" (p.xi). Again we see the perspective that there is a pure or natural mind within the writer that should be the focus of a teacher's nurturance; excessive directives on the part of the teacher will presumably alter or inhibit the natural course of the child's growth. What stands at the center of this perspective on learning is the primacy of the individual learner, with social considerations being secondary (and in the form of the teacher, often negative) influences on development.

The second assumption in *Inside/Out*'s title refers to the idea of *Developmental Strategies for Teaching Writing*. The book again implicitly draws on Piaget for theoretical organization. The developmental approach taken by the book is that at an early stage writers should begin with personal approaches to expression. Kirby et al. frequently describe the "natural" conditions that prevail in the approach to teaching writing that they take. In contrast, they point to the "artificial sequences" and "false assumptions and fruitless practices that underlie much of the teaching of writing in schools" (p. 5).

Tchudi and Tchudi describe "a major tenet of our philosophy of teaching reading: if you put kids in contact with relevant and interesting reading materials, *reading happens*" (pp. 77–78). Similarly, they claim that engagement with literature is "a natural process" (p. 81). Atwell too claims that certain behaviors occur naturally: "I never asked Hilary to relate her writing to her reading, nor sponsored exercises calling on kids to make writing-reading connections. It happens naturally, inevitably, in workshop settings" (p. 226). The writing that emerges naturally from the students described in these texts is almost inevitably of a personal nature, leading the authors to assume that personal writing is developmentally appropriate for their students, regardless of whether the students are in elementary school (Calkins), middle school (Atwell), high school (Tchudi & Mitchell), or college (Murray).

Often, personal writing is modeled for the students by their teacher. In Atwell's class, for instance, personal writing is greatly encouraged, from Atwell's own modeling of her own preferred mode of expression, to the content of the lessons she provides, to the exemplars of the professional writers that she offers. At times, then, it is not clear whether the students are doing what comes naturally to them or participating in the culture that the teacher creates in her classroom.

Student-Centered Pedagogy

The emphasis on a student-centered pedagogy is an extension of the developmental approach taken by the authors. Students are not "remedial adults," but adolescents with their own needs. In general, a pedagogy based on personal expression—primarily personal experience writing—emerges from the authors' sense of what a student-centered pedagogy ought to be.

In Tchudi and Mitchell's view of a student-centered pedagogy, "language will be learned when students are pursuing their own interests, and it is obviously difficult for teachers to know what those interests will be and when they will emerge" (p. 51). They say that

> If the teacher gives [students] confidence in their skills and a feeling of security about exploring new territory, they will, in the

end, at their own and natural pace, come toward the language behaviors identified by the "adult standards" model. . . . [I]f teachers will approach language from this student-centered perspective, the adult standards will be acquired in a much more solid fashion. (p. 52)

Tchudi and Mitchell attempt to "shift away from the conventional metaphor of the teacher as diagnostician and remedialist. Instead, the teacher may be a coach or catalyst, a resource person, advisor, or guide. Perhaps the best metaphor we have heard is that of the teacher as midwife—one who assists in the process of bringing something forth but who does not directly give birth herself" (p. 107). A teacher should not direct student learning, but help to guide it.

Tchudi and Mitchell favor teaching "writing as a process rather than product" (p. 193). Their conception of process is a "naturalistic" method in which "children learn to write by writing" (p. 207). They advocate journals, for which student response

has been almost universally positive, making it the closest thing yet to a surefire teaching device. . . . Many of the problems traditionally associated with writing seem to be almost magically solved when teachers use the journal. . . . We've come to realize that the journal "works" because it is closer to the "real" writing process than many academic writing assignments. (p. 195)

The "essence of the journal [is] its freedom and naturalness" (p. 196), they maintain.

Inside/Out offers an abundance of activities for teachers to use to help students make writing a more personal experience. The focus of the writing activities in the book is on *expressive* or personal writing. Most activities involve keeping journals, writing personal responses to literature, and producing creative writing based on personal experiences. When the focus shifts to expository writing, the authors attempt to get away from academic models of exposition and present a more personal approach, saying that "fine exposition grows out of imaginings" (p. 204). The sources they draw on are champions of personal, expressive writing: "Ann Berthoff, James Britton, Peter Elbow, Janet Emig, Donald Graves, Ken Macrorie, Nancy Martin, James Miller, James Moffett, Donald Murray, and Stephen Tchudi (Judy)" (p. 251). Kirby et al. celebrate the power of personal forums such as the journal, which they maintain is "an instant hit with teachers everywhere" and "the most consistently effective tool for establishing fluency" (p. 57) they have found.

Atwell's book is a conversion tale, a journey from teacher-centered assignment-giver to student-centered nurturer. At first, Atwell sits behind a "big desk" and prescribes instruction for her students. After meeting Donald Graves and Susan Sowers, Atwell repudiates such a role, "learning—and admitting—that I was wrong" (p. 4). As a "big desk" teacher, she had "assigned topics because I believed that my structures and strictures were necessary for kids to write well" (p. 6). Graves then convinced her that teachers should "look for and accommodate young writers' natural patterns of behavior." She comes to disdain "exercises, all those precious assignments that distance kids from natural, purposeful writing" and "book lists, all those genteel 'classics' that distance kids from natural, purposeful reading" (p. 21). Ultimately, says Atwell, "Now that I was freed from the constraints of my big desk, my kids would become my teachers" (p. 12).

The workshops Atwell suggests involve individual students pursuing personal goals. She says, "I mostly teach individuals, moving within the group to stop and confer with one writer or reader at a time. Because kids are writing on topics they've chosen and reading books they've selected, my teaching and their learning are about as individualized as they can get" (p. 45). In the workshop, "Each day writers will have a sustained chunk of time to go their own ways, writing and conferring; each day we'll come back together again at the workshop's end" (p. 86).

Atwell's reading workshop is similar to the writing workshop, with students involved in individual projects: "Except for the mini-lesson that begins reading workshop, there isn't any teacher to listen to and there isn't anything to do but read; the teacher reads too" (p. 160). All communication is done through dialogue journals. Says Atwell, "Although there's no talking out loud during the reading workshop, there's plenty of talking on paper" (p. 167).

Atwell gives almost exclusive attention to the personal narrative, with occasional attention to fiction and poetry as the optimal types of writing for middle school students. Atwell regards writing personal narratives as the "natural" mode of expression for her students, seeing it as developmentally appropriate for them.

Emphasis on Learning by Doing

The authors reviewed in this section advocate a "learning by doing" pedagogy that stresses experience rather than teacher-directed instruction. This approach is consistent with the idea that a classroom is a place that nurtures a child's natural path of development rather than having it directed by a teacher. As a result, there is little emphasis on instruction in strategies; most "teaching" is dispatched with quickly in order to get the students involved in the processes of reading and writing.

Tchudi and Mitchell offer an abundance of ideas on how to get students quickly engaged in activities. Many of the ideas they offer are excerpted from articles in the *English Journal* and *Notes Plus,* with many of the *English Journal* articles coming from Tchudi's tenure as editor. The evidence for the success of the teaching ideas is largely anecdotal or informal, often coming from suggestions given by teachers at workshops conducted by the authors. For instance, to address the problem of teaching literature, the authors offer the following:

> How does one avoid the many problems inherent in selecting and teaching common literary works to an entire class? Steve [Tchudi] asked a group of experienced teachers in a workshop at Michigan State University to write down their suggestions. Here is a selection of their responses. (p. 169)

The authors also draw on their own teaching experience to offer advice: "Diana [Mitchell] has used [children's books] in her urban high school classes, and thus we present them as yet another way to extend the books/young adult relationship" (p. 159). The teaching ideas are typically offered as something that has "worked" in a classroom, rather than as practices substantiated by formal research.

Tchudi and Tchudi's book grew out of a newsletter the authors originally published that responded to "a strong interest in how-to-do-it materials" (p. v). The activities come from the authors' own creativity, as well as "the common stock or 'lore' of bright ideas that are in circulation in our profession [and] students in methods classes, in-service days, and summer workshops" (p. vi). The book therefore has a strong orientation toward offering practical suggestions in the manner of *Notes Plus.* Ideas are addressed briefly, even those that are highly complex. For instance, Tchudi and Tchudi cover unit design in one chapter; they provide the reader "with a skeleton or outline, but it does not delve into the details of day-to-day teaching" (p. 35).

Tchudi and Tchudi avoid complex accounts of the learning process, suggesting instead how to create an environment in which students presumably will want to write. The book offers at one point "a potpourri of ideas for expanding the dimensions of literacy" (pp. 132–135) such as "have students write their name and personal slogan on a lapel button." The authors frequently represent complex ideas in capsule form. They tell readers, for instance, to "teach poetic form and devices as ancillary to meaning, secondary to interpretation" (p. 138). Actually implementing such a plan might entail a complete theoretical reorientation for many teachers, yet the authors present it in simple, accessible form.

For the most part, Kirby et al. and the sources they draw on also rely more on a practice-based inquiry than a research basis, and the book reflects a practitioner-oriented pedagogy with frequent nods to teachers who have given them good ideas. The activities they present are myriad, no doubt accounting for the great popularity of their book. With so many ideas to present, they tend to avoid presenting detailed instruction in specific aspects of writing and tend more to suggest to teachers how to put writers in potentially interesting situations.

Atwell's only intervention in her students' learning is through "mini-lessons," which are "five-minute presentations to introduce new concepts and techniques as I see writers need them" (p. 124). In the mini-lesson "the whole class addresses an issue that's arisen in previous workshops or in pieces of students' writing" (p. 77). Often, the problems are those that Atwell has in her own writing: "We all struggle with leads that will invite a reader's engagement, with dialogue that will express character, with the subtleties of transitions and the complexities of punctuation. In mini-lessons I share my own, professional writers', and students' real solutions to these real problems" (p. 78). Here, she reinforces the idea that the teacher is a learner in her own classroom; in her class, rather than playing the role of expert who can teach students more advanced skills and knowledge, "I begin to help when I look at my students as teachers who will instruct me about their lives" (p. 26).

Summary

The authors in this section stress a child's natural development and the need for a student-centered, process-oriented pedagogy according to psychological principles typically associated with Piaget. The teacher's role is to facilitate rather than direct student activities and development. Instruction is, by design, brief, with the assumption that students learn by doing more than by listening. The student's personal growth is stressed, with personal writing being the primary tool for learning.

The authors emphasize the primacy of the individual, though also acknowledge the importance of peer interaction. The peer interaction seems primarily for the purpose of giving feedback to help the student with personal response and expression, rather than being seen as a social force that contributes to the development of an individual's higher mental processes. This focus on the individual as opposed to a focus on the social environment of learning distinguishes the position we have just reviewed from several of the theories that we will now discuss. These other perspectives tend to stress the importance, and even necessity, of the transactional relationships among people that foster growth and development, with the idea of "natural" development a questionable conception due to the different ways in which people develop depending on the social and cultural environments in which they learn.

Transactional Theories of Literary Response

Required/Recommended

Andrasick, K.D. (1990). *Opening texts: Using writing to teach literature.* Portsmouth, NH: Boynton/Cook-Heinemann. [1/0]

Beach, R., & Marshall, J. (1991). *Teaching literature in the secondary school.* San Diego: Harcourt, Brace, Jovanovich. [11/2]

Nelms, B.F. (Ed.). (1988). *Literature in the classroom.* Urbana, IL: National Council of Teachers of English. [3/1]

Phelan, P. (Ed.). (1990). *Literature and life: Making connections in the classroom.* Classroom Practices in Teaching English, Vol. 25. Urbana, IL: National Council of Teachers of English. [1/0]

Probst, R.E. (1988). *Response and analysis: Teaching literature in junior and senior high school.* Portsmouth, NH: Boynton/Cook-Heinemann. [12/2]

Purves, A., Rogers, T., & Soter, A. (1990). *How porcupines make love II: Teaching a response-centered literature curriculum.* New York: Longman. [2/7]

Rosenblatt, L.M. (1938). *Literature as exploration.* New York: Appleton-Century. [1/9]

Simmons, J.S., & Deluzain, H.E. (1992). *Teaching literature in the middle and secondary grades.* Boston: Allyn & Bacon. [1/0]

Squire, J. (1964). *The responses of adolescents while reading four short stories.* Urbana, IL: National Council of Teachers of English. [1/0]

Sullivan, J., & Hurley, J. (1982). *Teaching literature inductively.* Anaheim, CA: Canterbury. [1/1]

Recommended

Corcoran, B., & Evans, E. (1986). *Readers, texts, teaching.* Portsmouth, NH: Boynton/Cook. [10]

Probst, R. (1984). *Adolescent literature: Response and analysis.* Columbus, OH: Merrill. [2]

Rosenblatt, L.M. (1978). *The reader, the text, the poem: The transactional theory of the literary work.* Carbondale: Southern Illinois University Press. [8]

Transactional theories of response to literature stem from Rosenblatt's two major works, *Literature as Exploration* and *The Reader, the Text, the Poem: The Transactional Theory of the Literary Work.* Transactional theories are typically pitted against New Criticism, which like Rosenblatt's theory had its prototypal work, Brooks and Warren's *Understanding Poetry,* published in 1938.

The contrast between the two approaches represents a number of conflicts in the field. New Criticism is typically regarded as teacher-centered, formalist, product-oriented, and content-oriented; the teacher's role is seen as authoritative, with the implication that the teacher is pre-scriptive concerning knowledge and dominant in terms of controlling classroom discourse.

Transactional theories, on the other hand, are concerned with the ways in which readers make meaning from their experiences with the literary text, thus making them more student-centered, meaning-con-structive, and process-oriented. The teacher's role is to help students construct meaning from texts, with the implication that the class should help students develop authority in their interpretations and contribute strongly to the construction of classroom discourse. To New Critical thought, the text is primary; to transactional theories, the text has no meaning without a reader. As Probst (1984) says,

> Rather than submit to the work, seeking only to find its "struc-ture of norms," the reader instead forces the work to submit to him. That is to say, he uses it, incorporating it into himself. He tests its perceptions against his own, not to bend to the vision it offers, but rather to take what he can from that vision in clarify-ing or enlarging his own. He approaches the text not as a disciple looking for answers, but as a thinker looking for possibilities. The individual work, then, is not an end in itself, but part of a longer process of building one's own picture of the world, a process that involves many books and many other experiences. (pp. 66–67)

The following sections outline the major premises of Rosenblatt's transactional theory of the literary work and the ways it is represented in the texts listed on the syllabi.

Transactional vs. Interactional Reading

To Rosenblatt, the transactional theory of the literary work "is simply an exemplification, with highly rarified complications, of the basic trans-actional character of all human activity, and especially linguistic activ-ity" (1978, p. 20). She distinguishes between a transaction and an inter-action, saying that an interaction implies a dualism between "separate, self-contained, and already defined entities acting on one another—in the manner, if one may use a homely example, of billiard balls collid-ing" (1978, p. 17). A transactional view, which she ascribes to Dewey and Bentley, designates "an ongoing process in which the elements or factors are, one might say, aspects of a total situation, each conditioned by and conditioning the other" (1978, p. 17). She repeatedly stresses the importance of the "essential dynamic interplay of particular reader and particular text" (1978, p. 171). She sums up the position by saying,

> Thus the transactional view, freeing us from the old separation between the human creature and the world, reveals the individual consciousness as a continuing self-ordering, self-creating process, shaped by and shaping a network of interrelationships with its environing social and natural matrix. Out of such transactions flowers the author's text, an utterance awaiting the readers whose participation will consummate the speech act. By means of texts, we say, the individual may share in the funded knowledge and wisdom of our culture. For the individual reader, each text is a new situation, a new challenge. The literary work of art, we have seen, is an important kind of transaction with the environment precisely because it permits such self-aware acts of consciousness. (pp. 172–173)

The transactional view, then, explicitly challenges the dichotomy between mind and matter typified by Piagetian approaches to learning. Rather than focusing on duality (as in the "inside out" approach taken by Kirby et al.), Rosenblatt says that "the concept of transaction emphasizes the relationship with, *and continuing awareness of*, the text" (p. 29). Similarly, Purves et al. (1990) propose "a response-centered program. It is not focused only on the students. Nor is it focused entirely on the literary works and literature. It's not subject-centered or student-centered. It deals with what happens when student meets subject. That way, it's student- and subject-centered" (p. 48).

The Constructive Nature of Reading

Another aspect of transactional learning concerns the constructive nature of communication. Beach and Marshall (1991) point out the shortcomings of the "transmission" model of communication that often dominates discourse in classrooms predominantly informed by New Critical pedagogy. In such classrooms, the teacher often provides an interpretive framework into which students slot information. When students cannot provide the missing information, the teacher-as-expert provides it for them, often assessing student acquisition of that information through a test. This conception of communication assumes that a sender (such as a teacher or author) transmits a message that arrives clearly and intact with a receiver (a student or reader); in other words, the text has a clear meaning that students receive, and the teacher provides an interpretation of that meaning that students receive without reconstruction. According to Beach and Marshall, this view does not take into consideration the inherent constructive, interinanimating nature of social and literary transactions.

Purves et al. see a need for changes in the relationships between students and teachers in a transactional setting: "The students are the explorers, but they need guides who help them, who warn them of dangerous swamps and alligators, who have scouted out the territory, who arrange for the food and shelter. The guide does not replace the explorer but is absolutely necessary to a successful exploration" (p. 63). Such guides are teachers who select and sequence texts, organize the class, provide additional information when needed, provide resources, guide talk, and give feedback. Students will need to learn how to teach, teachers will need to learn how to learn, feelings will count as much as intellect, talk should promote learning and response, and "reading inside the classroom will be a little bit more like reading outside the classroom" (p. 84). Response will become more open, including response through visual symbols, drama, oral interpretation, and hypertext, as well as more exploratory means of writing.

Focuses of Readers' Responses

As Beach (1993) has pointed out, "reader-response" theories such as Rosenblatt's transactional theory "embrace an extremely wide range of attitudes toward, and assumptions about, the roles of the reader, the text, and the social/cultural context shaping the transaction between reader and text" (p. 2). Beach (1993) identifies five focuses of attention among reader-response theorists: textual theories, experiential theories, psychological theories, social theories, and cultural theories. Rosenblatt (1938; 1978) is typically thought to have an experiential emphasis, with many theorists and practitioners who claim her influence focusing attention on the reader's past experiences and how the act of reading causes personal transformations.

Yet Rosenblatt's books are wide-ranging, giving extensive attention to all five focuses identified by Beach. The transaction between reader and text, then, is not simply a connection between the reader's attention to past experiences and the reader's perception of literary characters, but a wide range of processes encompassing the reader, the text, and the context of reading that result in a reader's construction of meaning. The following sections review each of the five types of transaction that Beach (1993) has accounted for in reader-response theories.

Textual. Some have argued that reader-response theories reduce texts to ink blots, with meaning residing only in the reader. While Probst (1988) argues that "a literary work has no significance at all until it is read" (p. 7), he also maintains that "the value of clear, accurate, correct reading is not denied, but affirmed. Such reading is achieved, however, only through careful attention to both text and self, through conscientious reflection on the thoughts and emotions called forth by the work" (p. 23). Rosenblatt (1938) concurs:

> *Fundamentally, the process of understanding a work implies a recreation of it, an attempt to grasp completely all of the sensations and concepts through which the author seeks to convey the quality of his sense of life. Each of us must make a new synthesis of these elements with his own nature, but it is essential that he assimilate those elements of experience which the author has actually presented.* (p. 133; emphasis in original)

According to theories that issue from Rosenblatt, then, the text is not an ink blot that stimulates only an inner vision, but a text in which an author has inscribed meaning conveyed through symbols, textual features, figurative language, and other literary devices. While different readers might have different associations with particular signs, they must all attend to the manner in which the author has crafted the signs.

Experiential. According to Beach and Marshall, an "intelligent" response to literature "involves the rich interplay of emotion and thought, of experiential knowledge (what we know because we've lived) and textual knowledge (what we know because we've read)" (p. 241). The personal experiences that a reader brings to a text are the factors most widely associated with reader-response theories, with Rosenblatt often cited as the source of this perspective. Rosenblatt (1938) argues that

> Since we interpret the book or poem in terms of our fund of past experiences, it is equally possible and necessary that we come to reinterpret our old sense of things in the light of this new literary experience, in the light of the new ways of thinking and feeling offered by the work of art. Only when this happens has there been a full interplay between book and reader, and hence a complete and rewarding literary experience.
>
> The work of art can have this effect, we have seen, because it does more than merely recall to us elements out of our own past insights and emotions. It will present them in new patterns and new contexts. It will give them new resonance and make of them the basis for new awarenesses and enriched understanding. (p. 127)

Beach and Marshall find that "schools do not usually begin their analysis of students by asking what they can already do well. The emphasis, rather, is most often placed on what students do badly or not at all. The curriculum is then conceived as a process of filling in gaps to remediate deficiencies or exposing students to new material" (p. 124). They argue instead that instruction should build on students' abilities and interests, should guide them toward a development of those abilities and interests (by means of instructional scaffolding), and should involve students in reflection on their own growth through educational activities.

For Probst, the transactional experience, when the reader is active and responsible, "enables the reader to remake himself. . . . Reading is an experience that shapes, perhaps confirming attitudes and ideas, perhaps modifying or refuting them. The student creates himself intellectually as he reads" (p. 24). An experiential approach, therefore, does not simply engender "an orgy of self-expression" or "an exercise in voyeurism" (Probst, 1988, p. 57) but an exploration that leads to greater self-understanding.

Psychological. Readers rely on psychological frameworks for interpreting what they read. Beach and Marshall refer to this as "topical" knowledge, with readers

> applying their background knowledge of different academic fields: literature, science, math, and second language, for instance; or topics: sports, politics, architecture, cooking, aviation. By applying their knowledge of these different fields or topics, students are learning, in Dennie Wolf's terms, to "read resonantly," to relate all of what they know to each new text. (p. 259)

A psychological perspective attempts to draw on relevant background knowledge in order to help readers make connections with texts. The knowledge concerns not only the facts that can inform reading, "but also a 'knowing-how' capacity to think like an historian, scientist, or artist. Applying these ways of thinking to literature helps students recognize that what they are learning in these courses serves to enhance their understanding of experience" (Beach & Marshall, 1991, p. 260). These "knowing-how" capacities are described in psychology as "schemata" or "scripts"—that is, the representations or frameworks that people develop in order to understand the processes of social behavior. People might have a script for a story genre, such as a detective story, to help understand the plot of a novel; they might also have schematic knowledge of personal experience, such as human hypocrisy, to understand *Gulliver's Travels.*

Social. Beach and Marshall devote attention to the manner in which classroom discourse shapes the ways students think about literature, citing a broad research base which includes their own. Their account of classroom process—particularly the patterns of discourse that prevail in discussions of literature—strongly affects the approach to teaching that they advocate. The authors examine the ways in which the social structure of the classroom influences the ways students learn. The social structure includes both the larger social influences, such as the ways in which classroom discourse affects students' thinking about their roles in the classroom and the ways in which they think about literature, and more immediate situations such as when a teacher "scaffolds" learning (*cf.* Bruner, 1975).

Beach and Marshall discuss the social consequences of taking a New Critical teaching approach, with its emphasis on arriving at a correct interpretation of the text, arguing that the roles of teachers and students will shape students' perceptions of how people think and speak about literature. They cite a typical teacher-led discussion in which

> The students' contributions to the discussion thus far are minimal. . . . Given the announced agenda, there is little students can do but follow the teacher's lead toward an interpretation of the story that is already beginning to take shape. They have few considered opinions about the story—they have only read it once—and thus they seem willing to listen as their teacher tells them what the story means. (p. 4)

In contrast to classroom discussions in which the teacher leads students toward a particular interpretation, Beach and Marshall advocate "the value of open-ended responses in the classroom" (p. 209). Therefore "students' responses on tests should be evaluated employing reader-based feedback in which the teacher describes the students' response processes. Rather than comparing students to a group norm, teachers should compare students against each other by noting changes in their performance over time based on a clearly defined set of criteria" (p. 220). They argue that only by changing the roles of teachers and students in classroom discussions, and by shifting the focus from reified expert interpretations of texts to the students' construction of meaning, will the social dimensions of reading literature empower students to have meaningful transactions with texts.

Cultural. Cultural factors that shape a reader's perceptions, orientations toward reading, and associations with particular signs in a literary text can also affect the transaction between reader and text. Rosenblatt (1938) maintains that the adolescent will already possess a wealth of culturally absorbed attitudes and ideas of human behavior. And it will be principally through this same process of unconscious cultural absorption that he will build up his images of the possible future roles that life offers. Innumerable influences in his environment will have given him a definite image, for instance, of the possible ways of behavior and feeling, even of the kind of temperament, appropriate or possible for a man or a woman. His parents and his family, through their own example and through explicit statement of the accepted attitudes, will have done much at an early point to set this mold. (p. 105)

As we will discuss later when reviewing sociocultural perspectives on learning, readers' cultural backgrounds may have important consequences for the ways in which they interpret the signs they find in literary texts or the ways in which they interpret the behavior of characters. *Huckleberry Finn*, for instance, which is regarded by New Criticism as an ironic work in which Huck's commentary on the humanity of blacks is viewed as contrary to what author Mark Twain believes, is often read as racist and offensive by black readers (*cf.* Smagorinsky, 1992; in press).

"Culture" extends beyond race, encompassing gender, religion, region, social class, and other factors that can shape a person's worldview. Beach and Marshall point out ways to help students take on cultural perspectives not typically assumed in classrooms. They argue that

In taking a feminist perspective, students are ultimately grappling with the question as to what constitutes a fully developed person, both as a female and as a male. But they are also beginning to learn about the gender-specific roles people often assume as members of a culture. Other kinds of cultural roles, of course, can also be explored. Students and characters often respond in predictable ways to the conventions of their communities, their region, their peer group, and the historical period in which they find themselves. All of these can be examined as part of a cultural perspective on literary texts. (pp. 258–259)

From this perspective, then, teachers should make an effort to make instruction "multicultural" in ways that go well beyond the inclusion of women and minority writers in literature anthologies. Rather, students' cultural backgrounds should be recognized as legitimate parts of their construction of literary meaning, and a range of possible constructions should be acceptable in the classroom not only for the purpose of democratic expression, but also for the purpose of enriching the perspectives of all students through engaging in transactions with students of varying orientations.

Emphasis of the authors on different focuses. The authors taking a transactional approach to literary understanding vary in the focus they emphasize. Beach and Marshall provide the broadest perspective, providing frameworks for textual, social, cultural, and topical knowledge as a way to teach literature. Probst and Purves et al. focus more clearly on experiential forms of response, with the reader's personal response to the text being of paramount importance. Purves et al., for instance, identify four objectives of a response-centered literature curriculum:

1. An individual will feel secure in his response to a poem and not be dependent on someone else's response. An individual will trust himself.

2. An individual will know why she responds the way she does to a poem—what in her causes that response and what in the poem causes that response. She will get to know herself.

3. An individual will respect the responses of others as being as valid for them as his is for him. He will recognize his differences from other people.

4. An individual will recognize that there are common elements in people's responses. She will recognize her similarity with other people. (p. 47)

Overall, the texts provide a balance of ways in which to consider the transactions that readers have with the literary work.

Efferent vs. Aesthetic Reading

Rosenblatt (1978) distinguishes between what she calls "efferent" and "aesthetic" reading. Efferent reading refers to what the reader will carry away from the reading, with the reader's attention "directed outward, so to speak, toward concepts to be retained, ideas to be tested, actions to be performed after the reading" (p. 24). An efferent reading of *Moby-Dick,* for instance, might include an objective test asking students to identify the roles of particular characters, or asking them to restate information from a teacher's lecture such as Shakespeare's influences on *Moby-Dick.*

In contrast, Rosenblatt describes aesthetic reading, in which "the reader's primary concern is with what happens *during* the actual reading event. . . . *In aesthetic reading, the reader's attention is centered directly on what he is living through during his relationship with that particular text*" (pp. 24–25; emphasis in original). An important part of an aesthetic reading is what she calls an "evocation" of the text. As Probst says, "To make anything of [literary images], students must first enjoy them as a performance. They must let the words conjure pictures for them, and then be willing to look at the pictures and allow their minds to wander in the scene" (p. 89). For Rosenblatt, these images become the subject of readers' interpretations:

> The tendency is to speak of interpretation as the construing of the meaning of a text. This conceals the nature of the reader's activity in relation to the text: he responds to the verbal signs and construes or organizes *his responses* into an experienced meaning which is for him "the work." This, we have seen, is a process in time. The reader ultimately crystallizes his sense of the work; he may seek to recall it or to relive different parts of it. (Have we not all recaptured episodes, characters, even speeches with voices reverberating in the inner ear?) All of this can be designated as the evocation, and *this is what the reader interprets.* Interpretation involves primarily an effort to describe in some way the nature of the lived-through evocation of the work. (1978, pp. 69–70)

For Rosenblatt, the lived-through experience of an aesthetic response is central to benefitting from a transaction with a literary work. To move too quickly to an efferent stance, as often happens with a New Critical approach to literature, denies the reader the experience of exploring the evocation upon which interpretation is based.

Summary

Rosenblatt's transactional theory, while often associated with the experiential perspective on response to literature, encompasses a broad spectrum of features of reader, text, and context. The authors from the syllabi who have appropriated her theory vary in the emphases they take. As noted, Probst and Purves et al. focus on the reader's personal response to the text. Beach and Marshall, in recommending ways to develop literature units, stress that students need to be involved in "learning to define connections" and thus "read[ing] resonantly" (p. 179). They suggest a number of ways in which to organize literature according to connections: topics, issues, themes, forms, genres, archetypes and myths, social or ethnic groups, and regions or settings. Beach and Marshall make a strong effort throughout their text to present the range of factors that are involved in transactions with literature, suggesting four different frameworks for designing instruction. Their goal is to show how texts can be taught "in a coherent, theoretically consistent fashion so that students may learn about the general processes of constructing meaning at the same time that they are learning the unique qualities of particular texts and genres" (p. 239).

Approaches Involving the Concept of Instructional Scaffolding

Required/Recommended

Flower, L. (1981). *Problem-solving strategies for writing.* New York: Harcourt, Brace, Jovanovich. [1/0]

Gadda, G. (1989). *Teaching analytic writing: An experimental study at the college level.* Unpublished doctoral dissertation, Indiana University of Pennsylvania. [1/0]

Hillocks, G., Jr. (1975). *Observing and writing.* Urbana, IL: National Council of Teachers of English. [2/1]

Hillocks, G., Jr. (1986). *Research on written composition: New directions for teaching.* Urbana, IL: National Council of Teachers of English. [1/3]

Johannessen, L., Kahn, E., & Walter, C. (1982). *Designing and sequencing prewriting activities.* Urbana, IL: National Council of Teachers of English. [2/0]

Kahn, E., Walter, C., & Johannessen, L. (1984). *Writing about literature.* Urbana, IL: National Council of Teachers of English. [5/0]

Lindemann, E. (1982). *A rhetoric for writing teachers.* New York: Oxford University Press. [8/0]

Smagorinsky, P. (1991). *Expressions: Multiple intelligences in the English class.* Urbana, IL: National Council of Teachers of English. [1/3]

Smagorinsky, P., & Gevinson, S. (1989). *Fostering the reader's response: Rethinking the literature curriculum, grades 7–12.* Palo Alto, CA: Dale Seymour. [1/3]

Smagorinsky, P., McCann, T., & Kern, S. (1987). *Explorations: Introductory activities for literature and composition, grades 7–12.* Urbana, IL: National Council of Teachers of English. [3/5]

Smith, M.W. (1991). *Understanding unreliable narrators: Reading between the lines in the literature classroom.* Urbana, IL: National Council of Teachers of English. [1/2]

Williams, J. (1989). *Preparing to teach writing.* Belmont, CA: Wadsworth. [1/0]

Zemelman, D., & Daniels, H. (1988). *A community of writers.* Portsmouth, NH: Boynton/Cook-Heinemann. [4/0]

Recommended

Hillocks, G., Jr., McCabe, B.J., & McCampbell, J.F. (1971). *The dynamics of English instruction: Grades 7–12.* New York: Random House. [5]

This set of publications offers a view of teaching and learning different from that presented in the section on "Piagetian Approaches Based on the Assumption of Natural Development." Indeed, on some occasions authors from this section deliberately contrast their position with that of authors from the first section. The authors in this section argue for a stronger role for the teacher in promoting student learning, with an emphasis on the design of activities that help students learn particular skills and concepts. The teacher's role is highly supportive at the outset of an instructional sequence and then diminishes as the students begin to demonstrate that they have internalized the principles of instruction. As in other approaches, the goal is for students to become more independent in their learning. In many ways, the authors in this section advocate the same form of pedagogy that Atwell abandoned when she left her "big desk" in order to let students direct their own "natural" course of learning.

The following sections review the main tenets of this perspective on teaching and learning.

Teacher as Teacher

Perhaps the most explicit challenge to the notion that development is a natural process that is adulterated rather than aided by adult guidance comes from Hillocks (1986). Hillocks's book is a lengthy research report on composition instruction from 1963–1983. From his aggregation of experimental research on classroom writing instruction, he offers a view of development that questions the likelihood that students' development is "natural," pointing instead to the ways in which teachers can accelerate and promote learning through the design of instructional activities. Teachers play less of the reactive, facilitative role described in the first set of publications and take a more assertive role in pointing student learning in a particular direction. Lindemann (1982) consistently refers to *assignments* that teachers prepare for students, an idea that is anathema to Atwell and others, saying that when employing the principles she advocates, "we can draft better writing assignments, specifying more than just a topic" (p. 17). In this conception, then, the teacher feels comfortable taking a leading role in students' learning. According to this approach, the teacher does not corrupt the students' natural path of growth, but helps provide knowledge and abilities to make the students' subsequent learning and experiences more productive.

Hillocks (1986) directs his attention to two general areas that teachers should attend to in planning instruction: "mode" and "focus."

Mode. A "mode" describes the roles and relationships between teachers and students in classrooms. He describes the mode frequently recommended by those predicating instruction on the assumption of natural development as "natural process" instruction (p. 119). He contrasts this mode with two others that predominate in classroom research. One is the "presentational" mode, which typically involves a teacher lecturing to students who are then tested on the given information. This approach to teaching is thoroughly reviled in virtually all of the texts assigned on the methods course syllabi, although by most accounts, it is the mode of teaching most widely practiced in schools at all levels.

The other classroom arrangement described by Hillocks is the "environmental" mode, which

> is characterized by (1) clear and specific objectives, e.g., to increase the use of specific detail and figurative language; (2) materials and problems selected to engage students with each other in specifiable processes important to some particular aspect of writing; and (3) activities, such as small-group problem-centered discussions, conducive to high levels of peer interaction concerning specific tasks. Teachers . . . are likely to minimize lecture and teacher-led discussion. Rather, they structure activities so that, while teachers may provide brief introductory lectures, students work on particular tasks in small groups before proceeding to similar tasks independently. . . . [P]rinciples [of learning] are approached through concrete materials and problems, the working through of which not only illustrates the principle but engages students in its use. . . .
>
> In contrast to the natural process mode, the concrete tasks of the environmental mode make objectives operationally clear by engaging students in their pursuit through structured tasks. . . . While the environmental mode shares an emphasis on process and student interaction with the natural process mode, it differs sharply from the latter in the structure of the materials and activities. (pp. 122–123)

An assumption behind this approach is that writing is a problem-solving process, a belief that is fundamental to the texts of Flower and Lindemann. Lindemann argues that "writing is a process of communication which uses a conventional graphic system to convey a message to a reader" (p. 11). This communication triangle of writer, subject, and reader "offers students a useful model for defining the rhetorical problem a writing assignment must solve" (p. 12). The types of problems that students solve are typically introduced by the teacher and are regarded by the authors in this section as applying to literature instruction as well as writing. For literature instruction, a teacher might give instruction in procedures for making literary inferences (Smagorinsky & Gevinson, 1989), with the assumption that such an ability is crucial for having satisfying experiences with literature.

Focus. The second area attended to by Hillocks is instructional "focus," which concerns the types of materials used by students to stimulate or guide their writing. Hillocks advocates what he calls an "inquiry" focus, which he says is congenial with specific topic suggestions and "tends to focus on immediate and concrete data of some kind during instruction and practice" (pp. 180–181). The inquiry focus "attempts to teach specific strategies" (p. 181) rather than letting students discover strategies in the act of writing. The focus of an activity can be quite varied, including a study of sea shells to improve descriptive writing (Hillocks, 1975), an analysis of brief "scenarios" (Johannessen et al., 1982) or longer "case studies" (Smagorinsky et al., 1987) to help students consider problematic situations prior to reading or writing, or the discussion of student-generated narratives prior to reading literature with a similar narrative structure (Smagorinsky & Gevinson, 1989).

Although Hillocks does not use the term "instructional scaffolding" (Bruner, 1975), the environmental mode seems to illustrate its principles well: The teacher provides initial support for student learning, then has students work with peers as a means of intermediate support, and finally has them work independently when they have shown signs of internalizing the knowledge they have been taught. As Applebee (1986) has pointed out, Hillocks's approach to instruction is one of many ways to scaffold learning, though it remains among the most clearly articulated. Development in this perspective is not "natural" but deliberately guided and explicitly instructed. This view assumes that the teacher knows more than the students and uses that more extensive knowledge to structure assignments that enable students to learn successful procedures (*cf.* Smagorinsky, 1986).

Time Allotted to Teacher-Led Instruction

One characteristic of this approach is the length of time students spend working at a skill or learning a new concept. As noted, the theoretical position based on an assumption of natural development endeavors to minimize teaching and get students involved quickly and extensively in the acts of reading and writing; the acts of reading and writing themselves serve as learning vehicles. Many of the practical texts produced in the tradition of Hillocks take a view that students need extensive instruction and practice in the subskills needed to perform a particular task effectively. These texts encourage teachers to conduct a "task analysis" to identify subskills and design instruction to teach them effectively. Although this characterization of this approach might sound atomistic, implying a "parts-to-whole" approach, effective instruction in this vein stresses the connection of knowledge with the parts serving the development of the whole.

In contrast to the mini-lessons offered by Atwell, for instance, Johannessen et al. devote an entire monograph to an extended unit of instruction covering roughly three to four weeks that focuses on learning how to write extended definitions. Students engage in extensive activities that involve them in thinking about definition problems prior to their actual writing of definition essays. Similarly, Smith (1991) describes a detailed set of lessons for teaching students how to judge a literary narrator's reliability, again covering several weeks of instruction and giving explicit attention to strategies for identifying five different types of clues in the text that can tip off a potential ironic narration, such as the contrast between Huck Finn's stated assessments of Jim's humanity and Jim's actual behavior toward other people.

Attention to Form

The authors grouped in the "natural development" section of this review find that the form of writing should be secondary to other considerations, such as how the learner's attitude toward reading and writing improve, how genuine a writer's voice and expression are, and what the student learns through the processes of reading and writing. The authors who believe in a teacher's stronger role share those concerns, but give greater attention to the formal properties of writing. Lindemann (1982), for instance, has written her book for college composition teachers who are often responsible for teaching students the conventions required to succeed in different disciplines. Attention to rhetorical concerns, then, becomes critical to her conception of writing instruction. She says that "when we use language in more formal ways, with the premeditated intention of changing attitudes or behaviors, of explaining a subject matter, of expressing the self, or of calling attention to a text which can be appreciated for its artistic merits, our purpose is rhetorical" (p. 37) and must take into account the discourse conventions appropriate to particular situations.

The attention to form does not come at the expense of attention to the writer's purposes. Rather, an effort is made to teach formal aspects of writing as a way to make one's purposes clearer to an intended audience. Johannessen et al. (1982) focus their monograph on extended definition, teaching its traits so that students may choose topics of their own to define and explicate. Kahn et al. (1984) give instruction in argumentation, again with the intent of teaching students strategies to employ in argumentation of their own choice. Without an understanding of the formal traits of written genres, students could falter in their efforts to communicate effectively with their intended audiences.

Summary and Caution

We should stress that the contrast we have made between the positions advocated by Hillocks and others and those believing in the natural development of children, while often sharp, is not absolute. Both reject lecture-dominated classrooms and present a process-oriented alternative. The texts are not absolutely divided on the issues of teacher-direction; Tchudi and Mitchell, for instance, draw on Tyler's (1949) model of curriculum development in their recommendation for unit design, a model similar to that found in Hillocks et al. (1971) and Smagorinsky and Gevinson (1989). And Lindemann freely draws on authors we have characterized as having a natural development orientation, such as Donald Murray, in developing her multiperspective on writing instruction.

In addition, many teachers of our acquaintance are not at all troubled by differences in epistemology. One of our favorite teachers in Norman, Oklahoma, names Atwell's *In the Middle* and Kahn et al.'s *Writing about Literature* as among her very favorite and most well-thumbed books about teaching. We contrast the different approaches because they rely on assumptions about development and the roles of teachers and learners that are quite different, particularly in the extent to which they do or do not move out from behind the "big desk." We suspect that many teachers see occasions when they should direct students' learning carefully, and occasions when it is more appropriate to let students work without structure and explicit direction. That the positions could be viewed by teachers as complementary, then, is not surprising.

Sociocultural Perspectives on Learning

Required/Recommended

Cleary, L.M. (1991). *From the other side of the desk: Students speak out about writing*. Portsmouth, NH: Boynton/Cook-Heinemann. [1/0]

Farr, M., & Daniels, H. (1986). *Language diversity and writing instruction*. Urbana, IL: ERIC Clearinghouse. [1/0]

Heath, S.B. (1983). *Ways with words*. New York: Cambridge University Press. [1/7]

Hynds, S., & Rubin, D.L. (Eds.). (1990). *Perspectives on talk and learning*. Urbana, IL: National Council of Teachers of English. [1/0]

Kutz, E., & Roskelly, H. (1991). *An unquiet pedagogy: Transforming practice in the English classroom*. Portsmouth, NH: Boynton/Cook-Heinemann. [1/6]

Perl, S., & Wilson, N. (1986). *Through teachers' eyes: Portraits of writing teachers at work.* Portsmouth, NH: Boynton/Cook-Heinemann. [2/2]

Power, B.M., & Hubbard, R. (1991). *Literacy in process: The Heinemann reader.* Portsmouth, NH: Boynton/Cook-Heinemann. [1/0]

Rief, L. (1992). *Seeking diversity: Language arts for adolescents.* Portsmouth, NH: Boynton/Cook-Heinemann. [1/0]

Rose, M. (1989). *Lives on the boundary: The struggles and achievements of America's underprepared.* New York: Penguin. [1/1]

Rubin, D.L., & Dodd, W.M. (1985). *Talking into writing: Exercises for basic writers.* Urbana, IL: National Council of Teachers of English. [1/2]

Shaughnessy, M.P. (1977). *Errors and expectations: A guide for the teacher of basic writing.* New York: Oxford University Press. [3/4]

Tannen, D. (1991). *You just don't understand: Men and women in conversation.* New York: Ballentine. [1/0]

Wigginton, E. (1985). *Sometimes a shining moment: The Foxfire experience.* Garden City, NY: Anchor. [1/0]

Recommended

Banks, J.A. (1984). *Teaching strategies for ethnic studies.* Boston: Allyn & Bacon. [6]

Mathieson, M. (1975). *The preachers of culture: A study of English and its teachers.* Totowa, NJ: Rowman and Littlefield. [2]

This perspective focuses on the socially and culturally influenced characteristics that individual learners bring to classrooms, attempting to account for the differences in performance by different cultural groups in school. The concept of culture refers to race in the eyes of many, but it also includes ethnicity, economic class, religion, region, and other factors that contribute to the cultural heritage of an individual. Sociocultural perspectives are often linked to theorists such as Vygotsky (1978, 1986), who posited that while people's biological mental processes tend to be similar, the "higher" or "sociocultural" mental processes developed among different cultural groups vary considerably. Vygotsky is often contrasted with Piaget, who stressed biological stages of development with social factors being secondary. Sociocultural research has looked at the ways in which people develop in a variety of cultures, not only according to their capacity for scientific operations but according to whether they view time as being linear or cyclical, how they are conditioned to participate in formal social situations, whether their primary means of communication is speech or some other form of mediation, and other facets of development.

Those taking a sociocultural perspective would probably take a different view from those operating from a position that stresses the "natural" development of children. According to a sociocultural view, people do not develop "naturally" but through the internalization of the patterns of thought and interaction practiced by the people around them. One of the main thrusts of this perspective is that schools tend to be organized according to the patterns of thought and interaction of the white middle class and that persistent patterns of failure, inappropriate behavior, and other presumed "deficits" of cultural minorities are attributable to differences between learned ways of thinking, knowing, and interaction rather than due to cognitive failure.

The following sections review some of the major tenets of the sociocultural perspective on learning.

Culturally Ingrained Orientations toward Literacy

Heath's (1983) book is among the most famous texts in modern sociocultural scholarship. She conducted a ten-year ethnographic study of a community in the Piedmont region of the Carolinas, focusing on three subcommunities: a white Christian fundamentalist community, a black lower-middle-class community, and the "mainstream" community of the town. Heath studied the ways in which young children were oriented to read in their homes and cultures, and then looked at the ways in which their reading orientations did or did not facilitate success in school. She found that the mainstream students engaged in practices at home remarkably similar to those practiced at school. When teaching their children something new, parents would pose questions to which they already knew the answers, initiating their children into the question/respond/evaluate patterns that predominate in elementary school classrooms, thus acclimating them to the patterns of discourse that lead to success in school settings.

In the fundamentalist community, the children were taught to hold the truth of the printed word in awe. Their early experiences with books came largely through reading the Bible, and they were taught to revere the inherent truth of the Biblical word. In school, however, they were required to interpret texts and often struggled with the demands. With the fundamentalist reverence toward the authority of the text reinforced continually in their world outside school, the children had difficulty adjusting to the demands of school reading.

The black community studied by Heath, on the other hand, was highly social and public in all its interactions. Reading quietly and privately was regarded as being asocial and was discouraged. When students from this community went to school, they were often regarded by middle-class teachers as being unruly, and their orientation toward reading penalized them in their efforts to succeed in school.

The work of Heath illustrates the importance of understanding the cultural backgrounds of students. The assumption that all students have followed the same natural path of development cannot account for their radically different, deeply instilled understandings of the purposes of reading and the norms for behavior in formal social settings that children of different cultures bring to school. Schools that expect a uniform set of outcomes from diverse students inevitably bias assessment in favor of those whose home environments most closely resemble the school environment, with the consequence that white middle-class students begin school with a great advantage that tends to grow into a wider deficit over the course of a twelve-year education, particularly in schools that "track" students. Because the performance of white middle-class students tends to get higher evaluations, teachers, community members, and the students themselves tend to believe that intellectual shortcomings, rather than incompatible practices of socialization, are responsible for differences in performance. The result of such thinking is harmful for all members of the community.

As an alternative, those taking a sociocultural perspective believe that classrooms need to be more open in the range of behavior accepted, the types of expression approved of, and the ways of knowing demonstrated by students, a reorientation that faces much opposition in the elephantine enterprise of school reform.

The Social Environment of the Classroom

Like Beach and Marshall, who report on classroom discourse and its effects on the ways in which students learn to think and talk about literature, Perl and Wilson (1986) (see also Hynds & Rubin, 1990) focus on the classroom environment and how it shapes the behavior of its participants. They conducted an ethnographic study of public school classes that employed teaching methods learned in a National Writing Project summer institute. They found that

> how teachers teach writing, or probably anything else for that matter, is a function of who they are, what matters to them, what they bring with them into the classroom, and whom they meet there. How they go about their work can be affected in certain important ways by conditions in the school, in the community, in the culture at large, but what affects teaching most deeply and

> dramatically are the themes, the interests, and the deeply felt concerns that affect and give shape to teachers' lives. (pp. 247–248)

In reaching this conclusion, they abandoned the notion that the teaching methods used by the teachers were accounting for whatever success the teachers were having, and tied the success of the classrooms to the convergence of students, teachers, school, and community, and the ways in which they acted together to create successful teaching and learning. Larger issues such as reflection and collaboration provided a better account for the processes they observed than the implementation of teaching methods.

The classroom, then, serves as a mini-community in which people of different backgrounds come together and forge a social compact that defines the ways in which people learn and communicate. As Beach and Marshall have pointed out, the imposition of a particular type of classroom discourse—the language of New Criticism—can have great effects on the ways in which students respond to literature and can make the likelihood for success much greater for students of some backgrounds than of others. Teachers need to be aware of the patterns of behavior and communication that they set up and of how their expectations affect the potential for success of a great range of students.

Attention to "Basic" Students

Sociocultural theorists have identified the needs of students who are classified as "basic," "remedial," or "at-risk" as central to their inquiry. Much effort in schooling has been devoted to bringing these students "up" to some acceptable level of basic achievement, with the measurement of success being their ability to speak and write "correctly." Those taking a sociocultural perspective try to build on what the students bring to class with them, rather than setting up a standard and expecting the students to meet it. As Shaughnessy (1977) says, her philosophy

> assumes that programs are not the answers to the learning problems of students but that teachers are and that, indeed, good teachers create good programs, that the best programs are developed *in situ*, in response to the needs of individual student populations, and as reflections of the particular histories and resources of individual colleges. (p. 6)

To Shaughnessy, a focus on the "errors" students make ignores the qualities that they may potentially develop. She says that

> When one considers the damage that has been done to students in the name of correct writing, this effort to redefine error

so as to exclude most of the forms that give students trouble in school and to assert the legitimacy of other kinds of English is understandable. Doubtless it is part of a much vaster thrust within this society not only to reduce the penalties for being culturally different but to be enriched by that diversity. (p. 9)

Both Shaughnessy and Rubin and Dodd (1985) offer practical suggestions for building on the language capacities that "basic" students bring to class, with Rubin and Dodd drawing on the dynamics of student conversation in small groups to help students talk through the ideas they will eventually write about.

In all cases the process of writing is viewed as long and necessarily including risks and mistakes that the teachers must encourage in order to help students overcome their fears of writing, most of which are grounded in the fear of error. When members of students' home communities speak in nonstandard dialects and the students are then expected to write "correctly" in order to succeed, they may never overcome their fear of performance and never develop as writers. Only by drawing on their linguistic resources and encouraging students to use them in their writing can teachers help students in the process of linguistic development.

Summary

The sociocultural perspective looks at the characteristics of the home and school environments that create particular types of literacy. Schools tend to value particular forms of thinking, social interaction, and expression that follow the patterns set in white middle-class homes. Sociocultural theorists are concerned with understanding better the literacy practices that students learn in their home communities and how those practices are and are not consonant with the behaviors expected of them in school. To make classrooms more sensitive to the abilities of a broad range of students in our increasingly diverse society, sociocultural educators urge teachers to reflect more on the social structure of their classrooms and consider how it affects the potential for success among students from different backgrounds. Ultimately, teachers are urged to open the range of response and expression so that students are not penalized academically for exhibiting culturally learned ways of knowing and interacting that are at odds with the structures of classrooms modeled on the values and patterns of behavior of white middle-class households.

Language as Process

Required/Recommended

Clark, V.P., Eschholz, P.A., & Rosen, A.F., eds. (1985). *Language: Introductory readings.* New York: St. Martin's. [1/5]

Corbett, E.P.J. (1992). *The little English handbook: Choices and conventions.* 6th ed. New York: HarperCollins. [1/0]

Farb, P. (1981). *Word play: What happens when.* New York: Knopf. [1/0]

Gucker, P.C. (1966). *Essential English grammar.* New York: Dover. [1/0]

Noguchi, R. R. (1991). *Grammar and the teaching of writing: Limits and possibilities.* Urbana, IL: National Council of Teachers of English. [1/1]

Pooley, R. (1974). *Teaching English usage.* Urbana, IL: National Council of Teachers of English. [1/0]

Strong, W. (1987). *Creative approaches to sentence combining.* Urbana, IL: National Council of Teachers of English. [2/0]

Tomkins, G. (1986). *Answering students' questions about words.* Urbana, IL: ERIC Clearinghouse. [1/0]

Weaver, C. (1979). *Grammar for teachers: Perspectives and definitions.* Urbana, IL: National Council of Teachers of English. [8/4]

Wells, G. (1986). *The meaning makers: Children learning language and using language.* Portsmouth, NH: Heinemann. [1/0]

Recommended

Andrews, L. (1993). *Language exploration and awareness: A resource book for teachers.* New York: Longman. [5]

Bean, W., & Bouffler, C. (1988). *Spell by writing.* Portsmouth, NH: Boynton/ Cook-Heinemann. [2]

Belanoff, P., Rorschach, B., Rakijas, M., & Millis, C. (1986). *The right handbook.* Portsmouth, NH: Boynton/Cook. [7]

Bernstein, T.M. (1967). *The careful writer: A modern guide to English usage.* New York: Atheneum. [3]

Butler, E., Hickman, M.A., & Overby, L. (1987). *Correct writing.* Lexington, MA: Heath. [1/0]

Fowler, H.W. (1931). *A dictionary of modern English usage.* London: Oxford University Press. [2]

Hodges, R.E. (1982). *Improving spelling and vocabulary in the secondary school.* Urbana, IL: National Council of Teachers of English. [3]

Larsen-Freeman, D. (1986). *Techniques and principles in language teaching.* New York: Oxford University Press. [1]

O'Hare, F. (1973). *Sentence combining: Improving student writing without formal grammar instruction.* NCTE Research Report No. 15. Urbana, IL: National Council of Teachers of English. [1]

Strunk, W., & White, E.B. (1959). *The elements of style.* New York: Macmillan. [2]

We have assembled quite a loose collection of texts under this category, all dealing with some aspect of the uses of language. Some take a prescriptive approach to language, providing accounts of proper style, syntax, and so on for speakers and writers to use. Some give attention to the problems associated with teaching grammar, providing alternatives for teachers who want or need to teach sentence structure, yet who are aware of the failure of formal grammar instruction. Unlike the previous perspectives, the theoretical positions of the books under this heading are not consistent in that some authors argue that certain elements of style are superior and are available to writers through the imitation of exemplary prose; others argue for greater emphasis on generative instruction such as sentence combining in which students view grammar and style as processes rather than as forms to be imitated.

Our discussion of these texts will not therefore attempt to account for a unified perspective on the usage of language. Rather, we will focus on the most widely used text, Weaver's *Grammar for Teachers* (1979), and use it to illustrate and contrast points made in other, less frequently used texts. Following are the chief points brought out by Weaver.

Problems in Defining "Grammar"

The study of grammar is highly problematic. For one thing, as Weaver notes, "The term 'grammar' itself is something of a chameleon, taking on different meanings in different contexts" (p. ix), with the definitions describing at various times syntax, usage, sentence structure, the processes by which sentences may be comprehended and produced, and a textbook that teaches all or some of these facets of language. The books that we have categorized under this perspective illustrate the range of definitions identified by Weaver, making any discussion of this issue necessarily diffuse.

The Documented Futility of Teaching Formal Grammar

Weaver emphasizes that instruction in formal grammar (such as that prescribed by Gucker, 1966, and Pooley, 1974) has consistently failed in instructional research to improve thinking, speech, or writing (*cf.* Hillocks, 1986). Weaver poses the question, "Why, then, do teachers continue to teach grammar?" (p. 4). Teachers, she says, are faced with an apparent contradiction. On the one hand, a considerable body of research and the testimony of innumerable students suggest that studying grammar *doesn't* help people read or write better (or, for that matter, listen or speak better either). On the other hand, the public in general and many English and language arts teachers in particular seem convinced that studying grammar *does* help, or at least it should. (p. 4)

The solution, according to Weaver, is that "students *do* need to develop a good intuitive sense of grammar, but they can do this best through *indirect* rather than direct instruction. Instead of formally teaching them grammar, we need to give them plenty of structured and unstructured opportunities to deal with language directly" (p. 5). She thus reinforces the idea that instruction should be dynamic and process-oriented, rather than focused on labeling of static elements of given sentences: "Language arts teachers and English teachers need, then, not only a knowledge of language structure (grammar), but an understanding of the language processes (listening, speaking, reading, and writing)" (p. 6).

Spurious Assumptions about Correctness

Weaver cites research in psycholinguistics to point out that the deep structures of language (those having to do with meaning) are more important, and better learned, than are the surface structures (those related to form). She points out that "we do not simply learn some underlying language structure and then automatically show equal proficiency in all of the language processes" (p. 13). Furthermore, "language learners often make errors that are a sign of progress rather than of regression" (p. 13), suggesting that much of the effort to force students into correct syntax may frustrate their attempts to control the more important deep structures of language.

The issues of dialect raised by the authors who take a sociocultural perspective are relevant to Weaver's points about correctness and are given attention in the collection edited by Clark et al. (1985). As reviewed in the section on sociocultural perspectives on learning, students are often treated as being intellectually deficient when their home dialects are at odds with the standard form of English prescribed by grammar books and spoken in most schools. Research in psycholinguistics characterizes the differences in dialects as differences in the surface structure of language rather than the deep structure, refuting the idea that speaking in a dialect represents a deficit in intelligence. Yet this persistent belief has pernicious consequences for speakers of nonstandard dialects in terms of teachers' expectations, teachers' assessments, and students' self-esteem.

Syntax and Reading

Weaver points out that "many readers do not seem to operate on the basic hypothesis that reading means getting meaning" (p. 54), instead reading words in isolation and failing to take into account the context of words and sentences. She argues that "there are various means of assessing students' ability to employ intuitive knowledge of grammar" (p. 54) to help them with their reading. In the long run, she says,

> the most helpful procedure may be to select literature with predictable syntactic/semantic patterns of various sorts and to give students explicit guidance in using such patterns as they read. Such assistance should help students become better able to use surface structure as a means of determining deep structure *and* better able to use deep structure as a means of determining surface structure. (p. 55)

Grammar and Writing

Weaver argues that evaluating writing through standardized assessments of mechanical skills should be avoided because

> (1) the use of such tests perpetuates the hypothesis that writing means producing written language that is superficially "correct"; (2) such tests tend to discriminate against those who speak a nonstandard dialect; (3) such tests measure little more than *one* broad aspect of writing, namely mechanics; and (4) there may be little correlation between scores on such a test and actual writing ability. (p. 85)

Like most theorists, she argues that students should learn to write by writing, rather than demonstrate knowledge about writing by taking tests on mechanics and usage. Attention to mechanics should come during revision, and even then should focus on a few details of mechanics rather than trying to correct everything all at once.

Weaver recommends indirect instruction in grammar rather than formal direct instruction from a grammar book. She recommends process-oriented approaches to teaching syntax such as sentence combining (e.g., Strong, 1987) as a good alternative, cautioning that such activities must be used only following the consideration of certain principles:

> (1) which kinds of exercises are appropriate for the students' level of development; (2) whether such exercises should cover a variety of syntactic constructions or only a few; (3) whether the

sentence combining should be done apart from normal writing, in conjunction with it, or both; (4) whether such exercises should be written or oral or both; (5) whether such exercises should be structured, unstructured, or both; (6) and whether to use technical terminology in the exercises or whether to teach mainly by example. (pp. 86–87)

Finally, Weaver maintains that "grammar needs to be combined with rhetoric; that is, students need not only to practice ways of combining sentences but to discuss which ways are more effective and why" (p. 87). The communicative purpose of writing should be a consideration of process-oriented exercises if the exercises are to help students with their writing; otherwise, the activities could be simply another form of busy work.

The Need for Teachers to Understand Grammar

Weaver stresses that although a knowledge of the formal labels given to grammatical parts is not necessary for students, it *is* necessary for teachers to have such a knowledge. Teachers are then "better prepared to help students avoid or correct certain kinds of problems with sentence structure, punctuation, and usage" (p. 90). The knowledge the teacher imparts is not static and prescriptive, but focuses "on process and on the active involvement of the student" (p. 94). An understanding of syntax can help a teacher help students to understand literature with unfamiliar structures, from e.e. cummings's poems, to Shakespeare's plays, to the dialects found in Zora Neale Hurston's *Their Eyes Were Watching God.*

A working knowledge of grammar, says Weaver, can inform instruction. The interest in grammar, however, must involve more than technological knowledge (see Farb, 1981). Teachers, she says,

> need to have a general interest in and excitement about language and its possibilities, an understanding of the language processes, and a respect for students' intuitive grasp of language structure. Such teachers will not dose their students with grammar, but rather engage students in using their language resources and expanding their ability to comprehend and use language well. (p. 97)

Summary

Grammar should be treated as a process, not as an artifact. Crucial to any treatment of grammar should be the deep structure of language in which meaning—not form—is the focus of attention. Teachers should take a more open-minded attitude toward dialects, building on students' linguistic resources rather than focusing on deviations from textbook-prescribed notions of correctness. "Errors" should be regarded developmentally rather than in terms of deficits. The study of language should help build a better appreciation of language and its possibilities, rather than focusing on the mechanical aspects of language that intimidate students into failing at and fearing language instruction.

Discussion of the Major Theoretical Positions

To frame our discussion of the major theoretical positions we have found in the syllabi, we will use the categories provided by a book we have not yet listed, Gere, Fairbanks, Howes, Roop, and Schaafsma's *Language and Reflection: An Integrated Approach to Teaching English* (1992), a book found on seven syllabi. Gere et al.'s book does not quite fit into any of our classifications; the purpose of the book, as the authors tell the reader in the introduction, is to "urge you to develop a theory of teaching" (p. vi). As such they do not so much advocate a particular approach to teaching as review the theoretical approaches available and ask teachers to develop a personal teaching philosophy that is informed by the frameworks they present. (Another recently published book taking a similar approach—that is, presenting theoretical positions for students to consider—is Daniel Sheridan's *Teaching Secondary English: Readings and Applications* [1993], which was cited in its prepublication manuscript form on one syllabus.) As a way of preparing for our own discussion of the theoretical positions we have reviewed, we will review the four perspectives that Gere et al. offer for teachers' consideration.

The first perspective that they identify is "language as artifact," which they associate with the formal study of grammar, New Criticism, cultural literacy, focusing on product over process, and an emphasis on the formal aspects of language. This perspective is rejected by virtually every text frequently assigned on methods course syllabi as being antiquated and working against any attempt to foster the personal growth of students—even though, as most observers of classroom practice (i.e., Applebee, 1993; Cazden, 1988) have found, the "language as artifact" approach continues to dominate much classroom process and assessment. Gere et al. nonetheless point out potential strengths of the approach: it develops cultural literacy, it permits measurement against a standard, it teaches close reading, it imposes intellectual discipline, it prepares students for college, and it affords flexibility. Its limitations, they find, are that it neglects the individual learner, the product is privileged over the process, students' writing is seen as mere exercises, analysis is stressed over other activities, texts become static, formula and format are stressed over creativity and individuality, it can present problems in motivation, and it places demands on the teacher as performer (pp. 97–99).

The second perspective they review is "language as development," a view that they associate with psychological accounts of language development. The group of authors we classified as using "Approaches Involving the Concept of Instructional Scaffolding" would fit into this category, as would those transactional theorists who take either a textual or psychological perspective. Such an approach focuses on metacognitive knowledge gained through direct instruction in learning procedures, particularly when that knowledge is scaffolded through teacher-led instruction. As Gere et al. point out, "Language-as-development teachers design a number of methods to help individual learners acquire the skills and strategies necessary to become effective in English classrooms" (p. 119). Gere et al. find that this perspective has a number of potential benefits for students: it assumes that all students can learn, it accepts the developmental stage of the learner, it makes learning strategies explicit, and it promotes successful imitation by students. They find it limited in that its view of sequencing is too often rigid and excessively linear, strategies are too often isolated from content, it privileges the literal over the interpretive, it privileges reading over writing, and it is apolitical and nonaesthetic (pp. 126–128).

The third perspective described by Gere et al. is "language as expression," which accounts for the two most widely represented theoretical positions found in the syllabi, the approach predicated on the notion of natural development and those transactional theories of literary response that focus on an experiential response. Gere et al. say that "the goal in this way of teaching is not to impart a certain set of facts but to enable students to trust their own responses; to understand why they would respond as they do; to respect the responses of others; to move beyond initial engagement to more sophisticated responses such as interpretation, evaluation, and construct-perception" (p. 146). Furthermore,

> Putting students at the center of the class means that the teacher becomes more of a facilitator than a performer in the classroom. Rather than serving as a single authority in the class, the teacher becomes an inquirer, one who sees students as co-inquirers who are capable of exerting their own authority in the learning process. (p. 149)

Gere et al. find that the strengths of this perspective are that it is student-centered, it celebrates individuality, it promotes independence, it promotes creativity, and it values feeling. It is limited because it privileges feeling over thinking, it is more individualistic than social, it privileges student texts and responses over professional texts and responses, it is time-intensive for the teacher, and it is loosely structured (pp. 158–162).

The fourth perspective Gere et al. identify is "language as social construct," a view represented in our analysis by the sociocultural position on learning, and also by the aspects of transactional theory that look at the social and cultural environments of learning. To Gere et al.,

> The language-as-social-construct perspective views language as a flexible, socially defined system through which humans negotiate meaning and understanding in their lives. It is above all social, constantly evolving, and generative. The role of the teacher becomes that of a more experienced peer who questions and clarifies in an effort to assist the student to reach more sophisticated and novel solutions or responses. (pp. 188–189)

The strengths of this perspective, according to Gere et al., are that it is student-centered, it promotes high expectations, it teaches critical, political, and social skills, and it is flexible. Limiting factors are that it is unconventional, teachers may have trouble administering it without administrative authorization, it privileges writing over reading and student texts over professional texts, it privileges the group over the individual, and it makes unusual demands on the teacher (pp. 194–196).

As noted, the authors have described these positions with the intent of distinguishing different perspectives for teachers to consider in making informed choices about their own teaching. Like the categories we have created in our own attempt to classify the field, we find their categories problematic at times. Central to the "language as development" perspective, for instance, is the notion of "instructional scaffolding," a concept that is most closely associated with the principles established by Vygotsky, to whom Gere et al. attribute the development of the "language as social construct" perspective. In making distinctions, Gere et al.—in the same manner as all who prepare typologies, including ourselves—create dichotomies that are not necessarily representative of the ways in which the perspectives are enacted in classrooms.

The limitations described for each section, for instance, are not, we feel, tempered by the ways in which a sensitive teacher might handle situations. Gere et al. identify being "apolitical" as a limitation of the "language as development" approach, yet Johannessen et al. include the definition of such inflammatory political topics as terrorism, freedom of speech, and cruelty to animals among the assignments in their monograph. The limitations Gere et al. identify therefore seem to be *potential* rather than real, and capable of being avoided through informed decision making. In spite of these reservations about *Language and Reflection,* we find it to be a useful book to help conclude our review of the major theoretical positions. We have presented our classification and analysis in order to report on the theories represented in the texts, rather than to make a case that any one should predominate. We would like to point out some contrasts that we find, though, and raise some questions about how those who teach methods courses can use theory effectively in their own courses.

We see the first theory that we describe, predicated on a belief in the natural development of children, to rest on assumptions about the nature of learning that are different from those underlying the theories that attend to social and cultural aspects of learning. To someone taking a sociocultural perspective—and here we include not only Shaughnessy and Heath but also Rosenblatt, and to a lesser extent Hillocks, whose focus on instructional scaffolding emphasizes the apprenticeship relationship between teachers and students—the idea of "natural development" is highly problematic. Children do not develop "naturally," they would contend, but are strongly affected by the language and other cultural influences in which they are immersed. Thus learners from different backgrounds entering the same classroom come with differently developed ways of thinking, knowing, interacting, and performing. The classroom itself also becomes a social environment that shapes the ways in which students learn to think and talk about their learning (*cf.* Marshall, Smagorinsky, & Smith, 1995; Smagorinsky & Fly, 1993). What happens in the classroom is not "natural," they would argue, but socially mediated and inherently part of a transactional, interinanimating relationship with the people and texts around them.

The question under dispute concerns the extent to which learning is primarily individual or primarily social. Atwell's account of her reading and writing workshops stresses the choice of individual topics and the development of a highly personal style of writing; her reading workshops, as she says, involve very little conversation. Kirby et al. declare in the title of their book that they perceive a difference between what is inside the writer's head and what is outside, stressing the dualism that Rosenblatt rejects in her transactional approach. The transactional, scaffolding, and sociocultural theorists we have reviewed characterize learning as a primarily social experience. The particular focus of the social influence varies from author to author, but the type of classroom that emerges from a social perspective seems to value collaboration and interaction as primary and essential vehicles for learning. We are *not* saying that the natural development approach eschews any sort of social interaction, or that the other positions suppress the individual; the purpose of the environmental mode described by Hillocks is to use social transaction as a scaffold for helping students to internalize strategies and concepts for individual application, and the texts written by Tchudi and Mitchell and others include sections on how to use group and collaborative activities. We make our distinction to point to the basic assumption about what is *primary* in each perspective's conception of learning, not what is exclusive to each perspective.

We see, indeed, how one could comfortably use seemingly contradictory texts cheek-by-jowl. Atwell's *In the Middle* stresses the empowerment of students through selection of topic and voice, an idea that could complement Beach and Marshall's notion that teachers should build on the linguistic skills and personal knowledge that students bring to school with them. Yet Atwell's book stresses individual, often silent, learning, while Beach and Marshall focus a great deal of attention on how to use talk effectively in teaching and learning about literature.

We have presented what we feel is the sharpest distinction we see among the different approaches taken in the texts students read in their methods courses. As we have said before, we find much in common even among the texts we see as being in greatest disagreement: All strive for learning that is constructive, student-centered, empowering, and meaningful. Identifying some key assumptions that separate them is important, however, if we are to take the perspective of Gere et al. and use this analysis to help those who teach secondary English methods courses to reflect on the decisions that they make about the texts they ask students to read.

Choosing textbooks for a syllabus presents interesting problems for instructors. We have seen courses that rely on a single text, often a large comprehensive book such as Hook and Evans's *The Teaching of High School English* (1982) or Tchudi and Mitchell's *Explorations in the Teaching of English;* we have seen courses in which an instructor assigns a range of texts that are theoretically consistent, such as Atwell's *In the Middle,* Kirby et al.'s *Inside/Out* and Tchudi and Tchudi's *The English/ Language Arts Handbook;* and we have seen courses that present texts that appear to be theoretically incompatible, such as Atwell's *In the Middle* and Beach and Marshall's *Teaching Literature in the Secondary School.*

We assume that the choice of books is made deliberately toward some end; that an instructor who presents conflicting theories does so either to provide a contrast, to present a range of choices for students, or because the books provide helpful ideas that might be suitable on different occasions. Like Gere et al., we would urge instructors to make the theoretical contradictions clear to students so that they make informed decisions in their own classrooms, and not just emerge from the methods class with a grab bag of ideas to use willy-nilly because they have worked for someone else in some other situation.

OTHER THEORIES AND ISSUES COVERED THROUGH READING ASSIGNMENTS

The syllabi gave less attention to the following issues. We provide the following lists as references for the books most frequently taught in each area. We list the issues in the order of their frequency of representation on the syllabi, beginning with the most often covered issue. Keep in mind that in some cases books from the following lists came from syllabi that supplemented the methods course, such as courses in young adult literature, the teaching of writing, and other areas.

The first issue covered includes more than ten texts. We did not include it under the heading of "Major Theoretical Positions" because it is a very loose collection of books that are designed to help acquaint students with either general classroom management procedures (i.e., Emmer, 1984), general teaching methods (i.e., Kindsvater et al., 1988), larger portraits of life in the teaching profession (i.e., Sizer, 1987), or cases for students to consider in anticipation of problematic teaching situations (i.e., Small & Strzepek, 1988). We will attempt no serious overview of the positions taken by these texts because the ground they cover is quite broad. We instead offer them as possible books to use should instructors find the issues covered in them worth sharing with their students.

General Teaching/Management/Survival Skills

Required/Recommended

Emmer, E. (1984). *Classroom management for secondary teachers.* Englewood Cliffs, NJ: Prentice-Hall. [2/1]

Freedman, S. (1990). *Small victories: The real world of a teacher, her students, and their high school.* New York: Harper & Row. [1/0]

Henson, K.T. (1988). *Methods and strategies for teaching in secondary and middle schools.* New York: Longman. [1/0]

Kim, E., & Kellough, R.D. (1974). *A resource guide for secondary school teaching.* New York: Macmillan. [2/0]

Kindsvater, R., Wilen, W., & Ishler, M. (1988). *Dynamics of effective teaching.* New York: Longman. [2/0]

Ornstein, A.C. (1992). *Secondary and middle school teaching methods.* New York: HarperCollins. [1/1]

Sizer, T. (1987). *Horace's compromise: The dilemma of the American high school.* Boston: Houghton-Mifflin. [1/0]

Small, R., & Strzepek, J. (1988). *A casebook for English teachers.* Belmont, CA: Wadsworth. [2/1]

Recommended

Bullough, R. *First-year teacher: A case study.* New York: Teachers College, Columbia University. [1]

Cooper, J. (Ed.). (1990). *Classroom teaching skills.* Lexington, MA: D.C. Heath. [6]

Emmers, A. (1981). *After the lesson plan: Realities of high school teaching.* New York: Teachers College, Columbia University. [3]

Evans, J., & Brueckner, M. (1992). *Teaching and you: Committing, preparing, and succeeding.* Boston: Allyn & Bacon. [5]

Froyen, L. (1988). *Classroom management: Empowering teacher leaders.* Columbus, OH: Merrill. [1]

Glasser, W. (1986). *Control theory in the classroom.* New York: Harper. [4]

Ornstein, A.C. (1990). *Strategies for effective teaching.* New York: Harper & Row. [4]

Postman, N., & Weingartner, C. (1969). *Teaching as a subversive activity.* New York: Delta. [1/0]

Reynolds, M. (Ed.). (1989). *Knowledge base for the beginning teacher.* New York: Pergamon. [2]

Williamson, B. (1988). *A First-year teacher's guidebook for success.* Sacramento, CA: Dynamic Teaching. [2]

Curriculum

Required/Recommended

Elbow, P. (1990). *What is English?* New York: Modern Language Association of America. [2/1]

Hillocks, G., Jr. (Ed.). (1982). *The English curriculum under fire: What are the basics?* Urbana, IL: National Council of Teachers of English. [1/1]

Hirsch, E.D., Jr. (1987). *Cultural literacy: What every American needs to know.* Boston: Houghton-Mifflin. [1/0]

Lloyd-Jones, R., & Lunsford, A. (Eds.). (1989). *The English coalition conference: Democracy through language.* Urbana, IL: National Council of Teachers of English. [1/1]

Mandel, B. (1980). *Three language arts curriculum models.* Urbana, IL: National Council of Teachers of English. [1/0]

Recommended

Davis, J.E. (Ed.). (1979). *Dealing with censorship.* Urbana, IL: National Council of Teachers of English. [3]

Farmer, M. (Ed.). (1985). *Consensus and dissent in teaching English.* Urbana, IL: National Council of Teachers of English. [4]

Glatthorn, A.A. (1980). *A guide for developing an English curriculum for the eighties.* Urbana, IL: National Council of Teachers of English. [3]

Mayher, J.S. (1990). *Uncommon sense.* Portsmouth, NH: Boynton/Cook. [1]

Simmons, J.S., Shafer, R.E., & West, G.B. (1978). *Decisions about the teaching of English.* Boston: Allyn & Bacon [2]

Squire, J., & Applebee, R. (1968). *High school English instruction today.* New York: Appleton. [3]

Tchudi, S.N. (1991). *Planning and assessing the curriculum in English language arts.* Alexandria, VA: Association for Supervision and Curriculum Development. [3]

Critical Thinking

Required/Recommended

Christenbury, L., & Kelly, P.P. (1983). *Questioning: A path to critical thinking.* Urbana, IL: National Council of Teachers of English. [3/0]

Golub, J. (Ed.). (1986). *Activities to promote critical thinking.* Classroom Practices in Teaching English. Urbana, IL: National Council of Teachers of English. [2/5]

Recommended

Marzano, R. (1991). *Cultivating thinking in English and the language arts.* Urbana, IL: National Council of Teachers of English. [3]

Neilson, A.R. (1989). *Critical thinking and reading.* Urbana, IL: National Council of Teachers of English. [1]

Small Groups/Conferences

Required/Recommended

Golub, J. (Ed.). (1980). *Focus on collaborative learning.* Classroom Practices in Teaching English. Urbana, IL: National Council of Teachers of English. [2/0]

Harris, M. (1986). *Teaching one to one: The writing conference.* Urbana, IL: National Council of Teachers of English. [1/3]

Johnson, D.W., Johnson, R., & Holubec, E. (1990). *Cooperation in the classroom.* Edina, MN: Interaction. [1/0]

Spear, K. (1988). *Sharing writing: Peer-response groups in English classes.* Portsmouth NH: Boynton/Cook. [1/0]

Recommended

Dawe, C.W., & Dorana, E. (1987). *One to one: Resources for conference-centered writing.* Portsmouth, NH: Boynton/Cook. [1]

Gere, A.R. (1987). *Writing groups: History, theory, and implications.* Urbana, IL: National Council of Teachers of English. [6]

Assessment

Required/Recommended

Cooper, C., & Odell, L., (Eds.). (1977). *Evaluating writing.* Urbana, IL: National Council of Teachers of English. [1/3]

Gronlund, N.E. (1991). *How to write and use instructional objectives.* New York: McMillan. [1/0]

Mager, R.F. (1984) *Preparing instructional objectives.* Belmont, CA: Lake. [2/1]

Myers, M. (1980). *A procedure for writing assessment and holistic scoring.* Urbana, IL: National Council of Teachers of English. [1/0]

Recommended

Anson, C. (Ed.). (1989). *Writing and response: Theory, practice, and research.* Urbana, IL: National Council of Teachers of English. [4]

Deiderich, P. (1974). *Measuring growth in English.* Urbana, IL: National Council of Teachers of English. [3]

Evans, P. (1985). *Directions and misdirections in English evaluation.* Portsmouth, NH: Boynton/Cook. [1]

Fagan, W.T., et al. (Eds.). *Measure for research and evaluation in the English language arts.* Urbana, IL: National Council of Teachers of English. [3]

Reading Comprehension

Required/Recommended

Johnson, D.D., & Pearson, P.D. (1984). *Teaching reading vocabulary.* New York: Holt, Rinehart & Winston. [1/0]

Vacca, R., & Vacca, J. (1989). *Content-area reading.* Boston: Little, Brown. [1/4]

Witte, P. (1985). *Guidebook for teaching reading.* Boston: Allyn & Bacon. [1/0]

Recommended

Berger, A., & Robinson, H.A. (Eds.). (1982). *Secondary school reading: What research reveals for classroom practices.* Urbana, IL: National Council of Teachers of English. [2]

Klein, M. (1988). *Teaching reading comprehension and vocabulary: A guide for teachers.* Portsmouth, NH: Boynton/Cook-Heinemann. [1]

McNeil, J. (1992). *Reading comprehension: New directions for classroom practice.* New York: HarperCollins. [4]

Computers

Required/Recommended

Rodriguez, R.R., & Rodriguez, D. (1986). *Teaching writing with a word processor, grades 7–12.* Urbana, IL: National Council of Teachers of English. [2/3]

Wresch, W. (1987). *A practical guide to computer uses in the English/language arts classroom.* Englewood Cliffs, NJ: Prentice-Hall. [1/0]

Recommended

Moore, P. (1986). *Using computers in English: A practical guide.* London: Methuen. [5]

Selfe, C.L., Rodriguez, D., & Oates, W. (Eds.). *Computers in English and the language arts: The challenge of teacher education.* Urbana, IL: National Council of Teachers of English. [2]

Wresch, W. (Ed.). (1984). *The computer in composition instruction.* Urbana, IL: National Council of Teachers of English. [2]

Rhetoric and Composition

Required/Recommended

Donovan, T., & McClelland, B. (1980). *Eight approaches to teaching composition.* Urbana, IL: National Council of Teaching of English. [1/6]

Graves, R.L. (Ed.). (1984). *Rhetoric and composition: A sourcebook for teachers and writers.* Portsmouth, NH: Boynton/Cook. [1/9]

Young Adult Literature

Required/Recommended

Donelson, K.L., & Nilsen, A.P. (1980). *Literature for today's young adults.* Glenview, IL: Scott, Foresman. [2/1]

Recommended

Abrahamson, R.F., & Carter, B. (Eds.). (1988). *Books for you: A booklist for senior high students.* Urbana, IL: National Council of Teachers of English. [3]

Carlsen, G.R. (1980). *Books and the teenage reader: A guide for teachers, librarians, and parents.* New York: Bantam. [3]

Gallo, D.R. (Ed.). (1985). *Books for you: A booklist for senior high students.* Urbana, IL: National Council of Teachers of English [1]

Small, R., & Kelly, P.P. (Eds.). (Winter, 1986). A critical look at literature worth teaching. *Virginia English Bulletin.* Virginia Association of Teachers of English. [2]

Writing to Learn/Writing Across the Curriculum

Required/Recommended

Applebee, A.N. (1981). *Writing in the secondary school.* NCTE Research Report No. 21. Urbana, IL: National Council of Teachers of English. [1/7]

Recommended

Britton, J., Burgess, T., Martin, N., McLeod, A., & Rosen, H. (1975). *The development of writing abilities 11–18.* London: Macmillan Educational. [7]

Fulwiler, T., & Young, A. (Eds.). (1989). *Language connections: Writing and reading across the curriculum.* Urbana, IL: National Council of Teachers of English. [5]

Gere, A.R. (Ed.). (1985). *Roots in the sawdust: Writing to learn across the disciplines.* Urbana, IL: National Council of Teachers of English. [6]

Langer, J.A., & Applebee, A.N. (1987). *How writing shapes thinking: A study of teaching and learning.* NCTE Research Report No. 22. Urbana, IL: National Council of Teachers of English. [3]

Mayher, J.S., Lester, N.B., & Pradl, G.M. (1983). *Learning to write/Writing to learn.* Portsmouth, NH: Boynton/Cook-Heinemann. [3]

Moffett, J. (1981). *Active voice: A writing program across the curriculum.* Portsmouth, NH: Boynton/Cook. [3]

Tchudi, S., & Yate, J. (1983). *Teaching writing in the content areas: Senior high school.* Urbana, IL: National Council of Teachers of English. [2]

New Criticism

Required/Recommended

Abrams, M.H. (1993). *A glossary of literary terms.* Fort Worth, TX: Holt, Rinehart & Winston. [1/0]

Perrine, L. (1988). *Story and structure.* New York: Harcourt, Brace, Jovanovich. [1/0]

Recommended

Dunning, S. (1966). *Teaching literature to adolescents: Poetry.* Glenview, IL: Scott, Foresman. [2]

Ideas for Classroom Practice

Required/Recommended

Carter, C., & Rashkis, Z.M. (1980). *Ideas for teaching English: The junior high and middle school.* Urbana, IL: National Council of Teachers of English. [1/0]

NCTE. (1984–1989). *Ideas plus: Books 1–7.* Urbana, IL: National Council of Teachers of English. [1/0]

General Textbooks

Required/Recommended

Bushman, J.H., & Bushman, K.P. (1986). *Teaching English creatively.* Springfield, IL: Charles C. Thomas. [1/0]

Hook, J.N., & Evans, W.H. (1982). *The teaching of high school English.* 4th ed. New York: Wiley. [3/4]

Teacher Research

Goswami, D., & Stillman, P.R. (Eds.). (1986). *Reclaiming the classroom: Teacher research as an agency for change.* Portsmouth, NH: Boynton/Cook-Heinemann. [1/3]

Formal Approaches to Teaching Writing

Marius, R. (1991). *A writer's companion.* New York: McGraw-Hill. [1/0]

5 General Discussion

We wish to open our general discussion of our study of undergraduate secondary English methods syllabi with a reminder of its limitations. Although we think that the syllabi can tell us much about the ways in which the courses are taught, they give us no idea of many of the most important factors that enable a methods class to provide a positive experience for preservice English teachers. The quality of the instruction provided by the instructors; the ways in which the course is situated in a larger teacher education program; the love of teaching that is engendered through the course: these and many other considerations are not revealed through a study of the documents that structure students' readings and responsibilities in the class.

A second important limitation is that the syllabi reflect the way the methods course was taught in a single year, 1992. Several instructors mentioned in their cover letters that they were in the process of revising their syllabi following their exposure to some new idea or book about the teaching of English. We can assume that many of the syllabi, if not completely overhauled, are revised from year to year to include new books, try new methods, adjust to new requirements, and otherwise grow with the field. Furthermore, since 1992, a number of new books about the teaching of English have been published (and of course many more will appear in years to come) with the likelihood that they will begin to appear on syllabi over the next few years. In a sense, then, our study represents a snapshot of the field rather than capturing its growth and direction.

Yet, in spite of the evolving nature of most course syllabi, we suspect that, as with much in life, the methods class represents the adage that *plus que ça change, plus c'est la même chose.* Many of the most frequently used books on the syllabi have been around for over ten years: Tchudi and Mitchell's *Explorations in the Teaching of English,* Tchudi and Tchudi's *The English/Language Arts Handbook,* Kirby et al.'s *Inside/Out,* Lindemann's *A Rhetoric for Writing Teachers,* and Weaver's *A Grammar for Teachers* were all originally published in 1982 or earlier, though the current editions of all except Weaver are revisions of the original texts. Atwell's *In the Middle* and Probst's *Response and Analysis* are relatively new among the most frequently used texts and both are over five years old. And still used in some courses is Hook and Evans's *The Teaching of High School English,* originally published in 1950 with the most recent edition in 1982. The longevity of certain texts speaks to a certain continuity in the methods course, even if the particular issues addressed are revised periodically to stay in step with the times.

We see too the likelihood that the approaches to teaching the methods class are fairly constant. Survey, workshop, theoretical, reflective, and experienced-based organization all sound very familiar to us through our experiences in the academy, and we doubt that we will see radical changes in these basic teaching approaches. While the specific content and processes might change with developing insights about the field, the roles, relationships, and responsibilities of instructors and students seem to fall into familiar types of patterns.

In spite of the limitations of studying course syllabi to gain information about the methods class, the documents do have a story to tell, even if that story requires some inference on our part. The syllabi give us a sense of what the overall approach and implementation of the course will look like, what students do and how they are assessed, and what theories students are exposed to in their orientation to the field. The syllabi give us a sense of the extent to which the methods courses themselves provide for their students the sorts of experiences that the theories which drive the courses recommend. And for those who are looking for different ways to teach the methods course, the syllabi have provided a cornucopia of ideas that could potentially improve the ways in which they teach their courses.

We have already provided extensive discussions of the implications of teaching approaches, assessments and activities, and theoretical orientations in chapters 2 through 4 and feel no need at this point to reiterate those arguments here. Our general discussion of the study will address two areas: the influence of the NCTE guidelines (Wolfe, 1986), and some general principles or "loose ends" that we would like to tidy up before concluding.

THE INFLUENCE OF THE NCTE GUIDELINES

The recommendations of the NCTE guidelines of 1986 (Wolfe, 1986) appear to have permeated, in one way or another, most of the syllabi we examined. But because only a few of the syllabi made specific references to the NCTE guidelines, we have no way of knowing the extent to which the professors designing the courses consciously attended to the guidelines or simply shared the same values as the NCTE committee and planned their courses accordingly. We would like to review briefly some of the points we have made along the way in presenting the teaching approaches, assessments and activities, and major theoretical positions found in the syllabi, using the framework from the 1986 guidelines to organize our analysis. We will next examine how each of the major tenets of the guidelines was reflected in the syllabi.

Student-Centered Classrooms

We found much evidence that the methods courses attempted to make learning student-centered, a concept that conjures up many different types of associations for different educators. For Atwell, a student-centered class is one in which the students take control of the curriculum and the teacher's role becomes one of learning more about the students' lives. For Hillocks, a student-centered classroom relies on the teacher to set up problems that students become actively engaged in so that they can become increasingly independent through metacognitive knowledge of learning procedures. For Rosenblatt, a student-centered classroom is one that values the personal construction of meaning through a transaction among reader, text, and context. For Heath, a student-centered classroom acknowledges the variety of culturally ingrained patterns of thought and communication of diverse students and strives to make the classroom more responsive to the ways in which individuals express themselves and demonstrate understanding.

We will not attempt to persuade our readers that any of these approaches is more student-centered than the others. Our point is that a class can be student-centered in more ways than one. The syllabi revealed many ways in which a methods class can be student-centered, though student-centeredness was always defined in the instructor's terms. In all cases the instructor set the agenda for what students would read and how they would demonstrate their understanding, of how they would spend their time and where they would focus their attention. Even in classes that we labeled reflective, in which students made choices based on their consideration of various theories and practices, the instructor determined the vehicles they would use to do so; while many might regard a learning log as a student-centered opportunity for reflection, we would point out that as a required assignment it issues from the instructor's agenda. In a sense, then, every course we examined was limited in the extent to which it was student-centered.

We are not troubled at all by this situation. We doubt that students in a methods class could inductively teach themselves about teaching, and so the agenda set up by instructors is, we feel, an important part of the experience that students have in their preservice education.

The question we would ask is: To what extent do the opportunities provided for the students enable them to reflect on and internalize the concepts presented by the course readings and other experiences in order to empower them to make good decisions in the classroom? The greatest potential we saw in the syllabi for giving students authority came through activities that encouraged their participation, in particular those that required transactions of some sort. Collaboration during learning (see chapter 3) appeared to provide excellent opportunities for students to use dialogue as a means of learning new concepts, with the instructor available for support if necessary. Many types of field experiences helped students make the transition from book learning to real-world applications, particularly when those experiences were scaffolded either by relationships with practicing teachers or by the dialogue of collaborators. Many types of reflection helped students tie their own personal learning experiences to the lessons of the methods class; as noted, these reflections could be formal, as in required journals, or informal, as in small-group evaluations of teaching plans.

The extent to which the methods classes themselves were student-centered might depend on how one defines the term. In our judgment, many of the classes provided opportunities for students to connect their own experiences and perspectives to the knowledge of teaching methods they were learning. Throughout our report we have described these practices at length and urge those who teach methods classes to consider them in their own planning.

Holistic Perspective

A holistic perspective, as we described previously, looks at learning as a whole-to-parts process that stresses the connection and continuity of learning. Only survey courses, which fragmented issues into discrete class sections, provided little opportunity for holistic learning. Other courses made some effort to get students to see connections among the ideas they were learning.

The particular focus of holistic learning varied, however. A workshop tended to look at the whole of an instructional unit as a worthwhile end for a methods class, with most of the course activities designed to get students to think of the overriding purposes to which all instructional decisions were subordinate. A theoretical course would try to get students to articulate the basis from which instructional practices issue, looking for a comprehensive grasp of theory. Reflective courses tried to present a range of theories in order to allow students to make informed choices about the direction their own teaching would take. Experience-based courses worked to tie together the worlds of theory and practice through close attention to what happens in real classrooms.

Again, each of these approaches has advantages, and each potentially has attributes that can—and often did in the syllabi we studied—apply to courses taking a different type of approach. The potential for holistic instruction in a teaching methods class appears great, with many options available to teachers and students.

Field-Based Experiences

Almost every syllabus we examined included some sort of situated learning. Roughly one-fourth included an actual field-experience component, although we do not know the extent to which field experiences were required in other parts of the preservice program and do not accurately know how frequently a methods course was paired with a practicum. We would say, though, that the idea of field experience was well-represented in the syllabi, most frequently in courses we labeled experience-based.

As we have argued, simply putting prospective teachers in the field is no guarantee that they will have good experiences or that they will become better teachers. Every teacher and university supervisor knows of disastrous relationships between preservice teachers and their mentors in the field. University supervisors always try to find good matches, yet they are not always possible.

In spite of this persistent problem, and in spite of the lack of research regarding whether or not field experiences actually benefit preservice teachers, we think that time spent in classrooms will surely be advantageous. For one thing, prospective teachers will get a chance to see how instruction actually works with real students, including those who don't do homework, those who fall asleep in class, those whose attendance is spotty, and those who otherwise challenge teachers. This touch of reality can help control the idealism that inevitably affects preservice teachers about the likelihood that their own sincerity and best intentions will win over even the most reluctant students.

Some other types of field experiences, we feel, can help preservice teachers get good preparation for the classroom. Directed forms of observation can help them understand patterns of classroom discourse, teacher expectations of students from diverse backgrounds, and the performance of particular "case study" students. Particularly, when students are given the opportunity to observe in pairs or to exchange their observations later, these experiences can help them gain a better understanding of classroom process and the ways that particular teaching methods work in particular classes.

Needs of Preservice Teachers

The NCTE guidelines made a noble effort to identify a great many specific needs of preservice teachers. Here we saw the greatest potential problem with their recommendations. As we discussed in chapter 2, the effort to satisfy too many requirements, to "cover all the bases," seemed to result in the fragmentation of the survey courses. We are not sure how to address this problem, in that we agree with much of what the guidelines say about the needs of preservice teachers. We would urge that while these goals should exist, those who prepare teachers should not try to satisfy all of them in a single course.

While choosing a particular focus for a course has its own disadvantages—such as precluding discussion of other, equally important concerns—the in-depth concentration on a few principles seems to benefit learning more than the brief coverage of many. The dilemma of "breadth vs. depth" is an old one in education that is exemplified by the problems we have found with survey courses. We are reminded of a high school colleague who taught a British literature course which she smilingly referred to as covering "from Beowulf to Virginia Woolf," an ambitious undertaking that always left her dissatisfied due to the limited time it left her for each work covered. We see the same problem affecting methods class teachers who believe that the recommendations of the NCTE guidelines—along with every mandate issuing from the state department—must be covered to the letter.

Models of Effective Teaching

The NCTE guidelines recommend that the methods class itself model the teaching methods advocated in the course. We found many examples of the modeling of effective teaching, which we reviewed in chapter 3. Reflective courses often began with syllabi that revealed the professor's reflective tendencies and proceeded to require students to reflect in journals, to connect their personal experiences to their anticipated teaching experiences, to engage in peer-response groups for their own writing, and otherwise participate in the types of activities that the course was attempting to teach them to use. Workshops involved a lot of small-group planning and feedback on the design of lessons and units, modeling the types of learning that presumably would work in the units students were preparing to teach. Experience-based courses tried to encourage collegiality through mentoring relationships with practicing teachers, required students to become careful observers of classroom process through observation logs and case studies, and gave attention to the design of instruction through feedback on teaching demonstrations. Theoretical courses required students to consider the motivating theories behind instructional practice, often through an empirical research base, thus helping to break down the barriers between research and practice. Chapter 3 provides an abundance of activities and assessments through which students can become involved in the types of learning that they may eventually encourage in their own classrooms.

Analysis of Effective Teaching

Students were required to analyze teaching in two settings, the field observations and the methods class itself. We have already reviewed several methods of analyzing teaching in real classrooms. In addition, a great many classes required students to put on teaching demonstrations for their classmates, at times videotaping them for future consideration. In virtually all cases, the teaching demonstrations were subject to peer feedback, thus giving the person putting on the demonstration a constructive critique and at the same time giving other students in the class opportunities to analyze teaching for its effectiveness.

Observation and Practice of Effective Teaching

We have discussed the observation of effective teaching. Many courses required teaching in two settings, the real classroom (as part of a field-experience component) and in teaching demonstrations for the class. Presumably, the feedback from peers and mentoring teachers would give the preservice teacher valuable advice that would make the transition from methods class to practice teaching a more comfortable experience.

Overall Effect of the NCTE Guidelines

The guidelines appear to have had a positive impact on the development of many methods classes. As we have said, we are not certain how often instructors consulted the guidelines and deliberately incorporated their suggestions into their courses. We do see great potential for building on the general principles and spirit of the guidelines in developing a methods class; the only danger we see is in trying to accomplish too much at once at the expense of covering the most important issues in depth.

GENERAL PRINCIPLES

Throughout our report we have described the possibilities for designing a methods course. We have endeavored first to be descriptive in order to characterize how instructors have conceived their courses and what they are having students do in them. Inevitably, we have been evaluative, using the NCTE guidelines as one source of judgment and our own set of criteria to judge both the syllabi and the NCTE guidelines themselves.

We wish to discuss at this point what we feel are some characteristics of exemplary syllabi that we have not yet attended to. The points we are about to make represent some lasting impressions that we have about the syllabi we studied and push a few points that we feel are worth making.

The Warmth of a Syllabus

One quality that we have not yet discussed, and one that is perhaps elusive, is the quality of *warmth*. Some syllabi that we examined opened with a personal message from the professor to the students. The message might be a personal introduction, an introduction to the purpose of the course, a welcome to the teaching community; but in each case the tone was inviting and reassuring, one that seemed to provide students with a good feeling about the class they were about to take and the profession they were about to enter. One syllabus, for instance, opened with some general information about the title of the course, the professor's office hours and telephone number, and a list of required texts, and then provided the following course description:

> As prospective English teachers, you already know a great deal about literature, about writing, and about general issues of teaching and learning. Research seems to indicate that what you know from your own classroom experiences has the greatest influence on the kind of teacher you will become. Many of you already have some strong ideas about what a successful classroom should be. This class will help you to discover/explore the ideas you already have and also expose you to new ideas—mine, your classmates', and those we read about. I am excited about the possibilities for rich exchanges of ideas.

This course has two primary purposes: (1) to provide an opportunity to articulate your vision of yourself as an English teacher and the implications of that vision and (2) to engage you in developing instructional theories and practices that will help you to enact that vision. We will explore what it means to be a teacher of literacy in the 1990s: not only the practical concerns of how to run a class, but also ethical and theoretical considerations.

This course will take theory into account and is predicated on the assumption that all teaching is based on theory—that *practice reveals theory.* English teachers reveal what they believe about the way language is best learned and the way knowledge is best constructed by the things they choose to do and choose to have students do. I believe you need the opportunity to develop and articulate a theory (*why*) you will teach in particular ways and then develop strategies (*what* and *how*) consistent with what you believe. Knowing why you do what you do will make you articulate in the job market and will enable you to become a lifelong learner of teaching and learning.

We remarked as we read this syllabus again and again how well it sets the tone for a class that we ourselves would like to take. The professor comes across as open-minded, caring, and knowledgeable, with a sense of authority that is at once reassuring yet not threatening. By introducing the course to her students in this way, the professor conveys a sense of the feeling the class will have and informs students of the overriding quality—reflective inquiry—that will make them good teachers. The course would go on to examine different methods of teaching, yet the introduction to the syllabus stresses the need for students to be careful thinkers about the ideas they would be getting from the course.

In contrast, some syllabi seemed cold and distant. Such syllabi—usually those we labeled surveys—often opened with massive lists of objectives, outcomes, and expectations, lists so long that they might be bewildering to a students as an introduction to a course. Or a syllabus might open with little introductory information at all, moving from a statement of purpose (sometimes a technical description from a course catalogue) to a list of assignments and textbooks to a list of the daily classes. Some syllabi were physically intimidating due to the choice of layout and font. For instance, one syllabus appeared in all capital letters in block paragraphs with both margins justified. The effect of these large blocks of print on us as readers was disconcerting, giving us the feeling that the course itself would be cold and inflexible. A few others used such a small font of print that reading the syllabus was a dense, uncomfortable, and fairly unpleasant experience, giving the impression that the course itself would follow likewise. While we don't wish to dwell excessively on this issue, we do feel that there is a relationship between tone (both the tone of the writing and the physical appearance of the syllabus) and content that is conveyed to students through a syllabus, one that affects their understanding of the professor's personality and of the approach to teaching they will learn.

We found that those syllabi that opened up with a warm introduction were often conversational and friendly throughout, suggesting that dialogue was an important part of the class. Of course, we cannot quantify this impression, but as impressions go, it was something we remarked upon frequently in our many readings of the syllabi. We often developed an affection for certain professors we had never met, simply through the tone of their syllabi, and suspect that students might have the same response.

Multiple Texts, Multiple Perspectives

Generally speaking, we found ourselves more impressed with courses that relied on a series of books rather than one or two. A series of books—and in some cases books accompanied by a collection of articles in a course packet—seemed to provide a broader, more flexible approach to teaching and learning than a reliance on a single perspective.

Here we will make an argument with which many people are likely to disagree. We feel that in order to emerge from a methods course theoretically informed, students need to read the theorists themselves, rather than getting the information secondhand and often sanitized in a general textbook. We think that it is significant for students to know who Rosenblatt, Applebee, Vygotsky, Hillocks, Murray, and other influential thinkers and researchers are and to read them in their own words. Textbooks tend to represent a general position such as "whole language" without going into the research base that supports it, the complexity of its implementation, and the theorists who question it. If students are to be theoretically informed about the decisions they make, then they need to come into contact with the people who are responsible for the theories they consider.

We see the importance of this type of knowledge in terms of an immediate understanding of the issues they are learning and also in terms of teachers' further growth in the profession. When seeing a reference to Applebee in an *English Journal* article, an informed reader can instantiate a network of understandings that is far more complex than it would be if the reader were unfamiliar with Applebee's clearly articulated positions on teaching and learning. The association of a name with an approach to teaching can be helpful in communicating with other teachers and in understanding articles in professional journals. An article that invokes Graves and Calkins in the opening paragraph, for instance, immediately tells an informed reader a great deal about the perspective the article will take. Readers who do not have knowledge of the research programs of particular scholars are at a disadvantage when attempting to understand new concepts or to grow through their reading of professional literature.

Perhaps we betray our academic bent in making this argument; undoubtedly some people would argue that students need the nuts and bolts of teaching without associating them with researchers and their theories. Yet, in order to grow professionally, teachers need more than nuts and bolts. If one of our goals is to be theoretically informed about the decisions we make as teachers, then an understanding of the origins of the theories we consider is essential. We urge English educators to consider the importance of the type of indoctrination that students get in a preservice program. If the program teaches them the importance of understanding the source of a knowledge base through an understanding of the people behind it, then we see the likelihood that they will see research as being conducted by people with beliefs and agendas and not simply accept (or, on the contrary, distrust) everything that comes their way preceded by "Research says. . . ." Through an exposure to multiple texts in a course (including articles in course packets), students are more likely to see how theories get developed and why it is important to continue to read professional material.

The Need for Inquiry

The final point we wish to make concerns the importance of encouraging inquiry among preservice teachers. By "inquiry" we mean the need to look into why classrooms work as they do. The developing field of "action" or teacher research shows great promise for helping teachers make inquiries into the implications of their own teaching. We see the preservice experience as being a great opportunity to orient teachers to the value of conducting classroom inquiries (*cf.* Smagorinsky & Jordahl, 1991).

Students undoubtedly learn not just methods but an attitude toward teaching in their preservice education. One attitude that we would recommend teacher educators to encourage is the need to continually monitor student learning through some sort of observation techniques. The observations could come through the data collected by classroom observers such as cooperating teachers or department chairs. The observations could come through self-analysis through videotaping or audiotaping classroom episodes. The inquiry could focus on the use of different teaching styles or methods in different sections of the same preparation.

Teachers who develop the habit of researching their own teaching early on in their careers could develop two important traits. First of all, they could become better teachers through the routine monitoring of the success of their own instruction. Second, they could be more knowledgeable about educational research, knowing which types they can trust to inform their own teaching. Teachers are notoriously wary of educational research for a variety of reasons. We see participation in the process of research as a way to help teachers become more knowledgeable about the potential of research for informing practice.

FINAL WORDS

This book has been designed for English educators to help acquaint them with the worlds of possibility available to them. We see our report as the beginning of a discussion that we hope will rely less on "lore" and more on more formal understandings of how and why we teach as we do.

In our conversation with our editor, Harvey Daniels, he suggested that we draw attention to the ways in which education courses are often dismissed by many reformers as a waste of time; the belief among many is that prospective teachers should immerse themselves in the content of their discipline rather than wasting their time learning teaching methods. We have chosen to end our lengthy conversational turn in the discussion of the methods course by mentioning this recurring argument, one that surely causes any professional educator to bristle. The field of education is simply not taken seriously by many citizens, including influential politicians, newspaper editorialists, practicing teachers who have taken uninspired education programs, professors across the university curriculum, and others who frequently voice their opinions on the matter. We believe that the education profession itself has exacerbated the problem by treating the methods course so lightly that we have little formal knowledge about the ways in which it is taught. We hope that this report will provide one way in which we as a profession can begin to discuss the teaching of preservice teachers as a meaningful, theoretically motivated, and important activity.

Appendix A: Five Neat Syllabi

In this appendix we present five syllabi that we feel are exemplary models for syllabus design. Our criteria for selection come from the arguments we make throughout this book regarding methods course development. The syllabus presented here is not necessarily the same syllabus that the author sent us in 1992, but rather represents a development in the way the course has been taught in the two years since. Aside from minor editing (such as the elimination of telephone numbers, which the teachers usually provide for their students—yes, home numbers, too) the syllabi we present here are identical to those distributed to students.

Syllabus 1

University of Wisconsin–Eau Claire
Curriculum and Instruction 358
Teaching Middle Level and Secondary English
Spring Semester 1993
Dr. Helen Dale

Office: 412 Hibbard	Office Hours
Office Phone: ———	10 M & W
English Office: ———	11 W
(to leave a message)	3 T & R
	and by appointment

REQUIRED TEXTS

Atwell, Nancy (1987). *In the Middle: Writing, Reading and Learning with Adolescents.* Portsmouth, NH: Heinemann. (purchased)

Gere, A., Fairbanks, C., Howes, A., Roop, L. & Schaafsma, D. (1991). *Language and Reflection: An Integrated Approach to Teaching English.* New York: MacMillan. (textbook rental)

Maxwell, R.J. & Meiser, M.J. (1993). *Teaching English in Middle and Secondary Schools.* New York: MacMillan. (purchased)

Perl, S. & Wilson, N. (1986). *Through Teachers' Eyes.* Portsmouth, NH: Heinemann. (purchased)

Short novel or play chosen by the class. (purchased)

COURSE DESCRIPTION

As prospective English teachers, you already know a great deal about literature, about writing, and about general issues of teaching and learning. Research seems to indicate that what you know from your own classroom experiences has the greatest influence on the kind of teacher you will become. Many of you already have some strong ideas about what a successful classroom should be. This class will help you to discover/explore the ideas you already have and also expose you to new ideas—mine, your classmates', and those we read about. I am excited about the possibilities for rich exchanges of ideas.

This course has two primary purposes: (1) to provide an opportunity to articulate your vision of yourself as an English teacher and the implications of that vision and (2) to engage you in developing instructional theories and practices that will help you enact that vision. We will explore what it means to be a teacher of literacy in the 1990s: not only the practical concerns of how to run a class, but also ethical and theoretical considerations.

This course will take theory into account and is predicated on the assumption that all teaching is based on theory—that *practice reveals theory*. English teachers reveal what they believe about the way language is best learned and the way knowledge is best constructed by the things they choose to do and choose to have students do. I believe you need the opportunity to develop and articulate a theory (*why*) you will teach in particular ways and then develop strategies (*what* and *how*) consistent with what you believe. Knowing why you do what you do will make you articulate in the job market and will enable you to become a lifelong learner of teaching and learning.

COURSE REQUIREMENTS

Subject to change dependent on both my and your assessment of your needs.

1. Regular attendance/Participation. We meet so infrequently that I really do expect you to be at each class session. Your grade will be lowered if you are excessively absent, primarily because if you are not there, you cannot participate. This is a professional class; it is for you and about what you know and need to know. Participation will count for approximately 15% of your grade.

2. A short (2–3 pages) teaching metaphor paper worth 10%.

3. A teaching perspective paper (3–5 pages) worth 20%. This paper should deal with theoretical concerns and how they would play out in your specific classroom.

4. Journals. You are expected to write at least twice a week. Date each entry. **Bring your journal to class each week for in-class** entries and also because I will collect them for grading without previous announcement. Journals will count for approximately 25% of your grade. Keep a separate section of a looseleaf notebook for these so that you can let me see just the pages that I have not yet read. The journals should be a response to the class and to the readings. After

class and after reading assignments, you should record your thoughts and your questions. Writing in your journal should prepare you well for class discussion. You might consider the following if you are stuck.

    a. What was the best/worst idea in this reading/class?

    b. How will what I have read/discussed affect my teaching?

    c. What points need to be clarified?

    d. What more would I like to know about this?

    e. Did I enjoy this class/reading?

A journal is informal by definition. Don't worry about spelling or other mechanical concerns. Just get your ideas down. What I'm looking for is a dialogue with you and a record of your thoughts and feelings as they develop and change. Feel free to ask me questions or direct comments my way. Don't feel you have to say what you think I want to hear. I'll read and evaluate them for content only. Honest. Grades will be based on effort and on the thinking revealed.

5. The final project, in lieu of an exam, is worth 30% of your grade. The project is to design a unit on the work the class chose and to spell out the specifics for three lessons: a before the unit (prereading) activity/lesson, a during the unit activity/lesson, and an after the unit (evaluative) activity or exam. You will probably cite some references. The last two class sessions, you will teach us one of your lessons or engage us in one of our activities.

FINAL NOTE

This course is absolutely noncompetitive. I hope you all get A's. There is no reason we shouldn't work together; in fact, on any of the assignments, should you decide to collaborate with another person, that's fine with me. That's especially true for the final project. Let me know of your plans and I'll give you some tips on collaboration.

This syllabus reflects my thinking before the start of the semester. The content is negotiable. This syllabus is only a plan, but I do not yet have specific students and specific needs in mind, and that context could make a big difference. We'll talk.

TENTATIVE COURSE OUTLINE/ASSIGNMENTS

* assignment due on that date

Week 1 1/19

    *No assignment

    -In class, Introduction to the course/ Classroom discourse/Discovering what we know and what we need to know/Selecting a novel or play that we can all read and on which we'll plan units.

Week 2 1/26

*In *Language as Expression,* read chs. 1–3, pp. 1–84.

*In your journals (a) address some of the questions on p. 45,

(b) on p. 69 address questions 11–14, and

(c) on p. 82 address the questions about your teaching metaphor.

-In class, we will talk about the issues in the three chapters.

Week 3 2/2

*In *Language as Expression,* read chs. 4 & 5, pp. 85–137 about the teaching perspectives Language as Artifact and Language and Development.

*Draft of your metaphor paper due

*In your journals, address your opinions and questions about the teaching perspectives.

*In *Teaching English* read ch. 4 "Selecting Literature" pp. 75–81 and ch. 7 "Improving Writing Skills" pp. 157–161 and 169–174.

*If you like, turn in a brief list of what areas of English teaching you would like addressed specifically in the course.

-In class, we will talk about these two perspectives on teaching English and we will have a short editing workshop to peer edit your metaphor paper.

Week 4 2/9

*In *Language as Expression,* read chs. 6 & 7, pp. 140–211 about the teaching perspectives Language as Expression and Language as Social Construct.

*Revision of metaphor paper due/Final Draft

*In your journals, address your opinions and questions about the teaching perspectives.

-In class, we will talk about these two perspectives on teaching English and discuss the four perspectives comparatively so you can think about which perspective most closely matches your own.

*In *Teaching English* read ch. 2 pp. 20–31 on classroom talk, ch. 3 pp. 49–56 on reader response, and ch. 5 pp. 107–122 on the writing process and journals.

Week 5 2/16

*Write a zero draft of your Teaching Perspective paper. (This is a draft to be read aloud or discussed—very rough)

*In *Language as Expression,* read chs. 8–10, pp. 214–284.

*In your journals, address

    (a) what you think it means to be literate,

    (b) what kinds of evaluation you prefer both for writing and reading assessment, and

    (c) what you think of tracking.

-In class, we will talk about the issues in the three chapters. I hope we will also have time for you to read and/or discuss your rough teaching perspective drafts with a classmate(s).

Week 6 2/23

*Read Atwell's *In the Middle.* (purchased book)

*Draft of Teaching Perspective Paper due.

*Once again I'd like you to turn in a list of topics related to English Education that you'd like me to cover before the course is over.

-In class, discussion of the possibilities and limits of workshop-type English classrooms and peer editing of the draft of the Teaching Perspective Paper.

Week 7 3/2

*Final Draft of Teaching Perspective Paper Due

-In class we will have a guest presentation by Richard Halle, a middle school teacher in Marshfield who runs a writing workshop with his students. Think of questions you might like to ask.

Week 8 3/9

* Read the selected chapters from *Through Teachers' Eyes.*

* In *Teaching English* read ch. 3 pp. 58–71 on pre-reading, reading, and evaluation activities, ch. 5 pp. 123–137 on different kinds of writing, and ch. 13, 299–333, "Developing Units Thematically."

* Journals will be collected for the final time

* Have decided before class a) whether you will collaborate with a classmate on your teaching unit and b) whether the fifteen minute activity you will do with the class will be a before, during, or after reading activity.

-In class, discussion of the teaching stories we read.

-In class we will decide who is presenting on 5/4 and 5/11.

-We'll spend much of the class talking about the teaching units. The more of the unit you have planned, the better we can help you evaluate its strengths and weaknesses and offer you suggestions.

Six weeks of teaching assisting/No class

Please feel free to see me about these units (or anything else) during the time you're out in the schools.

Week 15 5/4

*You may turn in your teaching unit today. If there are citations, which there probably will be, make sure to turn in a Works Cited List, either APA or MLA, but be consistent.

-Half of the class will teach a part of a lesson or activity from their unit. The rest of us will be 10th graders or whatever you want us to be. You set the context: place, grade, and ability level.

-Instructor Evaluations

Week 16 5/11

*FINAL DUE DATE FOR TEACHING UNIT. If you can turn this in before today, I'd really appreciate it.

-We'll meet this week so the other half of the class can teach their units.

Syllabus 2

Georgia State University
University Plaza, Atlanta, Georgia 30303-3083
Robert E. Probst, Professor of English Education

MEMORANDUM

To: Students in EDCI 450: "Clinical Teaching," Fall, 1993
From: Bob Probst
Re: Tentative plans for the course.

This course is intended to give students an opportunity to observe in the schools, to work with experienced teachers, and to meet and talk with students. I hope that such experiences will help you understand more fully the career for which you are preparing.

You will be taking EDLA 455 along with this course, and I hope that the two will be coordinated. The subject matter for both is the same—the teaching of English. If, in 455, I may lean toward the theoretical and ideal, in 450 I lean toward the actual and the practical. You will be placed in a school somewhere in the Atlanta metropolitan area and asked to observe and work with a teacher for about three weeks of the quarter. The schedule of visits to the school is being worked out now by the people responsible for placements, and it will entail visiting a school from about October 11th through October 29th. That should give you a coherent picture of at least several classes, since you will be in the schools 5 days a week, able to watch 2 or 3 classes move through about 3 weeks of instruction. Essentially what we are doing is stealing time from EDCI 450 during the first and last weeks of the quarter for EDLA 455, and returning it during the middle stretch for the sake of a coherent experience in the schools.

You'll be asked to keep a log of your experiences during the quarter, and perhaps to submit it occasionally for me to look through. The log should also provide you with thoughts, questions, concerns, hopes, fears, for us to discuss when we come together as a class in EDLA 455. Your reflections on what you observe and experience, recorded in this journal, will constitute the major effort for this course.

If your cooperating teacher agrees, you will be asked to work with individual students or small groups whenever appropriate, perhaps tutoring them, helping them with problems in writing or reading, or whatever else may be suitable. I hope, too, that you and your teacher will arrange for you to teach the full class for about four or five days. This teaching, if it can be managed in your situation, should be coordinated with the teacher's ongoing work and you might well rely heavily on her for direction. She probably will have planned the unit, will be able to tell you roughly what she would like you to do, and then you will be able to design the lesson plans for the days you teach. Ideally, you will pick up one day where the teacher has left off, carry the class for a few days, and then allow the teacher to resume.

The plans you prepare, along with a brief paper drawn from your log reflecting on the experience you have during the weeks in the schools will be submitted near the end of the quarter.

You'll also be asked to read and reflect on Mayher's *Uncommon Sense,* a book dealing with some of the significant issues facing English teachers today. We'll discuss this text as we discuss your experiences in the classroom, and it will inevitably come up in EDLA 455 as well.

Please see the remarks in *Random Comments on Papers and Prose* and the *Grading Policy* notes that should be appended to it. Those two documents express the general approach to evaluation. In this course, the major factors determining the grade will be:

> participation in the observations and teaching in the school;
>
> the log of observations and the paper summarizing your reflections on the experience;
>
> your plans for teaching for the week;
>
> your contributions to the discussion in our classes.

Please consult with me whenever you need to or want to during the quarter. (My office is 612 in the Education Building, the telephone number is _____ , and I'll often—though not always—be available during the several hours immediately following class.)

Miscellaneous Obligatory Comments

Prerequisite for this course is EDCI 452.

EDLA 455 is to be taken concurrently with EDCI 450.

Attendance policy—see the University *Catalog*. Regular attendance is expected.

Make-up examinations, if any examinations are offered, will be scheduled as soon as possible after the official examination date.

"The course syllabus provides a general plan for the course; deviations may be necessary." (*Faculty Handbook*, Georgia State University, January 1987, p. 47.)

———————

MEMORANDUM

To: Students in EDLA 455: "Secondary English Methods"
From: Bob Probst
Re: Tentative plans for the course.

The purpose of this course is to introduce you to the ideas, information, techniques, and resources that will be useful to you in preparing to teach English in middle, junior high, and senior high schools. It is intended to be a beginning, and as such it will leave you with more questions than answers. In so doing, it accurately reflects the state of the profession, which continues to investigate many basic and unresolved problems. Often during the quarter, we will find ourselves examining opinions, guesses, and suspicions, rather than facts, knowledge, and information. Our goal will be to acquaint ourselves with the thinking of the profession, incomplete as it may be, so that our decisions in teaching English may be as firmly grounded as possible in reason, or, at least, in instinct re-examined.

Not all of the work will be practical and immediately applicable to the classroom. There will be many discussions, I hope, that take us into the philosophical. If we don't have those discussions, then we will have neglected an important part of the course—a philosophy with no implications for practice is only useless, but a collection of activities or techniques with no philosophy to control and direct them may well be dangerous.

Tchudi's *Explorations in the Teaching of English*, third edition (Harper and Row), is the basic text for the course, with Mayher's *Uncommon Sense* serving both this course and EDCI 450. Tchudi's book should serve as an adequate introduction to the issues we'll be considering. You might also want to pick up his *The English Teacher's Handbook* (Winthrop, 1979) or some of the other compilations of teaching ideas.

The bibliographies in Tchudi, along with the catalogs of the National Council of Teachers of English and Boynton/Cook-Heinemann, should get you well started into related readings. I'll leave you on your own to select most of that other reading, but I'll be happy to advise or assist anyone who requests some other suggestions. You should, of course, acquaint yourself, as quickly as possible, with the appropriate journals. *The English Journal* and *The Journal of Reading* will be among the most useful for you now.

Teaching

Much of our class time will be spent in discussion of your reading, but we will also experiment with some of the techniques the texts and articles will recommend. It will be an imprecise simulation at best, but lacking the opportunity to bring a high school group into the classroom, we will have to satisfy ourselves at first with some practice within our own group. These trial runs will be opportunities to experiment within a group that ought to be encouraging and supportive. For those of us beginning teaching, they will be opportunities to have a fairly comfortable experience controlling a group and instructing, and for those of us who have taught before, they may be chances to try out ideas, perhaps to experiment with techniques or content.

We'll work out the details for these teaching sessions fairly soon and I invite your suggestions—much of what I say at this point is tentative and may have to be changed. Each of us will teach one lesson. The person teaching the lesson will be responsible for preparing the plan, teaching, reviewing the lesson with the class, and revising the plan accordingly. Those serving as students—all the rest of us—will be responsible for performing in that role, and for offering criticism and suggestions at the conclusion of the lesson. We'll allow about 45 minutes for the teaching, and about 15 minutes more for the discussion of each lesson, though we may have to modify this schedule depending upon the number in the class.

There are foreseeable problems, the most troublesome of which is that the lessons will take a great deal of time and there is much to read and discuss. We should begin these soon, so there is little time to immerse ourselves in the reading before we begin the teaching. Nonetheless, it seems essential in a methods class to try our hands at teaching, and so we will live with the compromises. Assuming about 20 students in the class, we'll need to devote quite a few sessions to the presentations. I'll work out a tentative schedule.

Units and Lesson Plans

Although, in this scheme, you'll be asked to teach only once, you will need to prepare a unit of instruction that covers several weeks. These units should attend to all of the four areas (oral language/group dynamics, literature, composition, language) that serve as the organizing categories for the course and should include about ten complete and thorough lessons. If you have an idea that doesn't seem to fit a category, however, use it regardless—this classification shouldn't bind you. For these lessons and units there are countless models. See especially those in your texts, in Loban, Ryan and Squire, and in Hillocks's *The Dynamics of English Instruction.* There are a number of other good methods texts—I'll show you some—and they will also have suitable examples.

As you prepare your plans, please keep in mind that they have to communicate to others. They will therefore not be as brief and telegraphic as they may become at some later time in your career, when you have more experience and less obligation to inform others about your intentions for the classroom. They may be longer, too, than those you will write when you have to plan for five periods a day, five days a week. Here you have only ten or so plans to prepare, as part of your unit, for an entire quarter and so you should, insofar as possible, make them exemplary.

The unit and its lessons will be your major obligation for the course. I'll discuss this in more detail later, but it is essentially a plan to cover a sequence of related lessons covering about four weeks. Here again there are some good models in your text and others. The unit plans in Spann and Culp's *Thematic Units in Teaching English and the Humanities* are for the most part good and might serve as models. I would like to have your units reproduced and distributed to the class, though the budgeting crisis will probably require us to finance such an undertaking. We will have time during the class to work on the units, probably meeting as groups to encourage the exchange of ideas. And we'll also take some time near the end of the course to present them to the class.

Some questions for us to consider: Should we plan for a range of both grade and subject matter, or allow complete freedom of choice? Should we insist upon a uniform format for all plans?

Schedule

I've worked out a tentative schedule, which follows, for the readings in the early part of the course, but since we are working on a new class schedule this year, I'll leave much of the quarter up in the air at the moment. This does not represent all the topics I'd like to consider during the course. Nonetheless, it may serve as a rough outline of the course, one that I will feel free to adjust as seems desirable. Often, we'll find that issues arise in the discussion unpredictably—we'll probably let the talk take its own course rather than constrain it rigidly by this schedule, even though that will at times seem chaotic.

During the first several weeks, we'll borrow time from EDCI 450 for the sort of work usually associated with 455, compensating later in the quarter (roughly October 9–November 8) with uninterrupted time for observations in the schools. This will allow you to observe several classes a day, 5 days a week, which will give you a somewhat more coherent picture of the teaching than you would otherwise get, and it should still give equal time to each of the two courses. **Keep in mind that this schedule will have to be modified continually as the quarter progresses.**

In addition to the reading recommended here, there will be additional suggestions.

Week One, 9/20–24: Background.
    Tchudi, chapters 1, 2, 3, 4, 5, 16
    Wilkinson, "The Concept of Oracy," *English Journal,* January, 1970.

Styles and Cavanaugh, "Language across the Curriculum—The Art of
Questioning and Responding," *English Journal,* February, 1980.

Week Two, 9/27–10/1: Problems of instruction in literature.
Tchudi, chapters 6, 7, 8, 13
Howell, "Unlocking the Box: An Experiment in Literary Response,"
English Journal, February 1977.
"Enlarging the Range of Response," *English Journal,* February 1977.
Duke, "The Case of the Divorced Reader," *English Journal,* February 1977.
"Close-Up: Adolescent Literature," *English Journal,* February 1975.
Donelson, "Censorship in the 1970's," *English Journal,* February 1974.
Blake and Lunn, "Responding to Poetry: High School Students Read
Poetry," *English Journal,* February, 1986.
Squire, "The Current Crisis in Literary Education," *English Journal,*
December, 1985.
English Journal, February 1979.
English Journal, March 1977.

Week Three, 10/4–8: Problems of instruction in composition.
Tchudi, chapters 4, 9, 10
Kantor, "Research in Composition: What It Means for Teachers,"
English Journal, 70(2), February 1981.
Smith, "Myths of Writing," *Language Arts,* 58(7), October 1981.
Larson, "Discovery Through Questioning: A Plan for Teaching Rhetori-
cal Invention," *College English,* 30(2), November 1968.
Murray, "Write Before Writing," *College Composition and Communication,*
29(4), December 1978.
Arbur, "The Student-Teacher Conference," *College Composition and Com-
munication,* 28(4), December 1977.
Tchudi, "Writing for the Here and Now," *English Journal,* 62(1), January
1973.

Beginning on about the 11th, we'll be in the schools.

Weeks Four–Seven, 10/11–10/29: In the schools, approximately 9:00–12:00.

Week Eight and Nine, 11/1–16: Presentation and discussion of lessons and units.

Week Ten, 11/23: Final discussions, final examination (tentative).

Please keep in mind that this schedule is virtually certain to change as
we learn more about the placements and schedules for the visits to the schools
that you'll be engaged in with EDCI 450. You may receive several versions over
the next weeks.

I don't yet know how to schedule the other topics I'd like for us to cover
and still have time for the presentation of your units—we'll have to see how it
works out. Some of the following issues will probably be addressed repeatedly
during the course:

Nature of the adolescent.

Importance of language in conceptualizing experience.

Students from minority and ethnic groups.

Students with special educational problems.

Considerations in the planning of instruction.

Values and concepts in English instruction.

Planning.

Lessons, Units, Courses, Programs.

Materials.

Texts, Films, Tests, Equipment.

Thinking.

Critical, Imaginative, Problem-solving.

Special techniques.

Creative dramatics, Guided fantasy.

Organization of schools.

School politics.

Public pressures.

Working conditions.

Teacher rights and responsibilities.

Please raise the questions that interest you. The class need not bind itself to a rigid and unvarying outline of topics. We'll rely on the expressed judgments of the class to help make decisions about the content and the procedures for our work. Similarly, I will rely on individuals to keep me informed about their problems or concerns. Please consult with me whenever you need to or want to during the quarter. (My office is 612 in the Education Building, and the telephone number is _____, and I'll often—though not always—be available during the several hours immediately following class.)

Evaluation

Please see the remarks in *Random Comments on Papers and Prose* and the *Grading Policy* notes that should be appended to it. Those two documents express the general approach to evaluation. In this course, the major factors determining the grade will be: the unit plan, the lesson taught in the class, the contribution to the discussions of teaching, any examinations that may be offered.

Miscellaneous Required Comments

EDCI 450 is to be taken concurrently with EDLA 455.

Attendance policy—see the University *Catalog*. Regular attendance is expected.

> Make-up examinations, if any examinations are offered, will be sched-
> uled as soon as possible after the official examination date.
> "The course syllabus provides a general plan for the course; deviations
> may be necessary." (*Faculty Handbook,* Georgia State University, Janu-
> ary 1987, p. 47.)

RANDOM COMMENTS ON PAPERS AND PROSE

You may find many of the following comments unnecessary, and some so obvious that they border on the offensive, but since the problems to which they are addressed arise regularly in papers, I thought that it might be helpful to offer a few suggestions. Among the standard and traditional recommendations for papers you'll find several that are idiosyncratic—those I mention simply to inform you of my own biases and preferences, not to obligate you to share them.

Subject and Conception

1. First of all, choose a subject that demands and provokes thought. Deal with an idea, an issue, a problem, a possibility. For the paper to be substantial, the issue attacked must have substance. Summaries, lengthy paraphrases, and lists are seldom worth the trouble. Don't undertake a project that will result in such a list or collection—such projects lack the coherence that makes them readable. The project should have a narrative or expository thread that holds it together. Don't, for example, annotate a collection of books—if the books hang together well enough to allow a cohesive paper, that's fine, but if there isn't a sufficiently unifying theme, choose another topic. The summarizing and paraphrasing that you do undertake should lead somewhere, make some point, contribute to some analysis.

2. Identify an issue that matters to you. Spend a week reading and reflecting; then choose a topic that intrigues you, or that is significant in your work. A topic chosen because it seems easy, or simply because there's a book at hand dealing with it, is likely to yield a perfunctory essay.

3. As early in the quarter as possible, survey the material available on the topic, so that you can complete the necessary research.[1] If a crucial article is unavailable in our library and must be borrowed from Stanford, you will

---

[1] The most common problem with the research supporting papers received is that it is simply inadequate—the writer has examined too little of the potentially useful material—and that often seems to be the result of waiting until the third or fourth week of the quarter to begin. Another is that the research is often undigested. It is simply presented, summarized, and then forgotten while the writer moves on to talk about his own ideas. The writer must relate the research to his own thinking if it is to serve the paper.

need weeks, rather than days. Check the bibliographies and indexes early, perhaps with the help of a reference librarian, so that you don't have the unhappy experience of discovering that the time you spent in the Modern Humanities Research Association's *Annual Bibliography* should have been devoted to *Psychological Abstracts*.

Conferences

4. Because the paper is usually the single most important task in the course, I strongly suggest that you confer with me about it. Ideal would be a conference near the beginning of the quarter as ideas are forming (but after you've put some thoughts on paper, both for yourself and for me, since conferences are seldom useful without something in writing to refer to), another—the most important—during or shortly after drafting the paper, and a final conversation after the work is polished. The conferences aren't mandatory, and I will neither demand them nor even request them (except here)—the responsibility for setting up the conferences lies with the student—but without them there is absolutely nothing I can do to assist you during the writing, to encourage you, to forewarn you of possible problems, or to help you evaluate the results of your labors. I should note, also, that although they may serve some purpose, brief exchanges in the hall immediately before or after class seldom constitute much of a conference.

5. In the early conference my role is to assist you, if I can, perhaps simply by listening to your ideas, perhaps by suggesting lines of inquiry, references to consult, other questions to consider. The main reading of the paper—the one that I hope will enable me to make suggestions and offer some guidance—should be at about the fifth or sixth week of the quarter, by which time the draft should be well along. I'd hope that this reading will enable me to see clearly what the paper will accomplish and what problems may be arising, and I'll try to comment on the draft in as helpful a way as I can.

   It seems important that I be able to read this draft, not simply hear about it. Often, when students read sections of manuscript to me, explaining what they intend to do, both problems and possibilities are obscured. For instance, the writer may refer to a great many authorities, suggesting that the research is thorough, but I may be unable to see, without a text in hand, that the citations, numerous though they may be, haven't been assimilated, digested, and directed effectively toward the issue of the paper. Or, in a unit plan, a student may report that he'll have a series of discussions around a certain theme and I'll envision a planned sequence of questions, only to find the cryptic instruction to "discuss." I've found that conferences undertaken without having actually read a draft of the paper can be very misleading, both for me and for the writer.

   My role in the last reading of the paper, and in the final conference, is simply to evaluate and to grade (for further comments on grading, see the *Notes on Grading Policy in English Education Courses*).

6. Although I may jot down some remarks on your drafts or your final paper, or in an attached note, these will seldom be more than brief reminders, for

me, of issues to discuss in the conference. Without a conference you may find them obscure and difficult to interpret. I've found it far more efficient to talk with students about their papers, and so I don't usually indulge in lengthy written comment, especially on the final version, where written remarks are least useful. My hope is to be helpful and honest and tactful. If, as often happens, I'm unable to achieve all of those goals, I'll try at least to be honest.

Since the most time-consuming reading of the paper should be of the draft at about the fifth or sixth or seventh week, the final draft will probably not be due until the week before class ends, or possibly even the last night of class, depending on the circumstances of the quarter. This final reading will be done quickly since its major purpose is not to yield suggestions, which it will now be too late to implement anyway, but simply to arrive at an evaluation and a grade. Any comments I make at this point in the quarter will be very brief, ranging from "Excellent—send it to the *English Journal*," to "We probably both wish now that we'd had that conference three weeks ago." It would be desirable, however, especially if you'll wish to confer about the final draft, for me to have it the week before it's due, since that will leave us more time in which to schedule a meeting. Obviously, the more time I have with the paper, the more careful attention I can give it and the more likely we are to be able to find a mutually agreeable time to confer. As you plan your work for the quarter, keep in mind that the last weeks of the quarter are hectic, and that conferences may become difficult to schedule. Papers will probably not be accepted after the last class session and if, for some reason, they are, they'll be considered during what is usually the busiest week of the quarter, which means that there will barely be time to glance *at* them, much less *through* them.

I prefer not to extend the conferences into the following quarter, unless they are about a paper with extraordinary possibilities.

Format

7. Don't worry about format during the first two or three drafts—I'll be happy to confer with you about anything I can read easily. Before you prepare the final draft, however, look over this document and make sure that you follow its guidelines. I feel no obligation to read final drafts that don't conform to these specifications.

8. This document illustrates some, but not all, aspects of the format. The paper should have a title page, set up as illustrated in the sample attached. Page one should have your name, address, and phone number in the upper right. Subsequent pages should have your name and a page number. Do not, under any circumstances, forget to number your pages. Footnotes and bibliographies should be handled as illustrated using numbers, not asterisks. If your paper is unusually long, let's say 50 pages or more, you may begin numbering again with each new chapter; otherwise number consecutively throughout. Type the paper, one side only, on paper of substantial weight, not onion-skin, using a reasonably fresh, dark ribbon. If you cannot, for some reason, type or have the paper typed, see me.

9. Double-space, except for those quotes and lists that you choose to set off and indent—I single-space here because these notes are to be reproduced in large quantity. The margins should be roughly what they are in this document—about one inch all around. You need not hyphenate words to even the lines, but do not right-justify text unless you are willing to hyphenate extensively and have a printer that handles microspacing well. Even then I'd prefer that text not be right-justified.

10. Proof-read the paper. I admit it's a bit stuffy, but I don't appreciate creative spelling or avant-garde sentence structure, and won't read beyond the third or fourth error that a competent seventh-grader with a dictionary could have eliminated. Clear, idiomatic prose is expected. (I'm referring here, again, to the final, polished, edited draft—don't let worries about these matters interfere with earlier drafts.)

11. Staple or paper-clip the pages in the upper left-hand corner and nowhere else—don't weigh down my brief-case with unnecessary pounds of metal along the sides or the top. Don't fold the papers. They should be unbound or in a file-folder—*nothing* more ornate. No green cardboard notebooks with flowers sprouting from the spine, no blue styrofoam boxes with birds perched on the lids, no yellow cellophane with chartreuse plastic strips, no ring-back binders, no complicated straps or snaps or clips or contraptions.

12. Consult a style manual if you have questions, Turabian's, preferably.[2] The MLA manual is also fine. APA is terrible, the most inconvenient and cumbersome of them all. I know, however, that many journals require it, and I've about given up hope of consigning it to the warmer circles—use it if you must. Whatever you use, be sure that it calls for *complete* information about the source, when it is first cited, on the same page as the footnote call.

13. Be sure to give appropriate credit to your sources. The consequences of plagiarism, intentional or accidental, are catastrophic.

14. Keep a carbon of your paper. This is especially important if the paper is likely to be exchanged by mail at some point.

15. If you prefer to hand in the work on disk, it will have to be in IBM format—unfortunately, I'm not equipped to handle the Apple format disks.[3] Please be sure that the disk has free space remaining, at least twice the amount of space occupied by the text file. The final draft should probably be in hard copy.

---

[2] Kate L. Turabian, *A Manual for Writers of Term Papers, Theses, and Dissertations,* 4th ed. (Chicago: University of Chicago Press, 1973). Or the 5th edition which, I believe, has recently been released.

Evaluation

I don't propose to bind myself tightly to a scheme for evaluating papers. Subject, purpose, style, available information, and all other aspects of the writing will vary too widely to allow for an inflexible set of criteria. Fiction, unit plans, videotapes, and computer programs, for example, would have to be evaluated on their own terms. The following matters, however, will be significant for almost any genre you might undertake in these courses:

Focus and Conception: Is the subject of the paper clearly identified? Is it an issue worth writing about? Is the purpose evident? Does the paper deal with an idea? Does it present an adequate conception of the problem or the issue?

Research: Has the writer consulted appropriate and adequate sources? Does he understand the other work that has been done on his topic? Does he use the related work effectively in building his argument, avoiding simple summary? Does the paper reflect current knowledge, professionally accepted principles and practices? If it recommends departing from accepted standards, does it argue intelligently and persuasively for that departure?[4] The unanswerable question of length always arises—my experience has been that it's difficult to offer enough in fewer than 10–15 pages, and that it's hard to hold interest for more than 25–30. There have been many exceptions.

Organization: Is the paper well-arranged? Is it divided into suitable parts, suitably related to one another? Does the paper move to some conclusion or resolution?

Thought and Logic: Is the paper well-argued? Is it reasonable? Does it provide evidence that leads to its conclusions or generalizations? Does

---

[3] As long as it's readable by an IBM computer, the disk may be either 3.5" or 5.25", either standard double-density or high-density. I'd prefer that the file be prepared in WordPerfect or WordPerfect for Windows. Microsoft Word, Word for Windows, Lotus Manuscript, Ami Pro, and WordStar are also fine. I think that I can convert CEOWrite, MultiMate, DisplayWrite 2 or 3, Samna, Sprint, Volkswriter, Wang PC, WordMARC, WordStar 2000, or DEC WPS PLUS. If, however, any of those will allow you to export files—preferably in DCA/RFT, otherwise in simple ASCII code—please do so. If you've prepared it with PC-Write, Bank Street Writer, or Term Paper Writer, I may be able to figure it out, but I'd prefer the exported file. If you use some other processor, you'll have to export in DCA/RFT or ASCII or turn in hard copy.

[4] Most courses will recommend a core of reading, and that reading will probably represent at least some of the current thinking on the subject. Most papers should reflect an awareness of that material, but that does not mean that they must accept the assumptions, conclusions, and beliefs represented in that reading. If a writer wishes to reject currently accepted notions, however, he should do so consciously, with careful justification for his purpose.

it provide sufficient detail, enough illustration, to make its points clearly and persuasively? Is it creative, innovative; does it offer insight?

Language: Is the prose clear, idiomatic, precise, and correct? Is the style appropriate and pleasant? Is the paper legible, readable, in acceptable form? Has it been carefully proofread to eliminate mechanical errors?

I don't intend to suggest a hierarchy in this brief list of criteria and won't try to specify the weight each criterion will have in the final evaluation. It should be obvious, however, that a paper must be satisfactory on some criteria before others will have any bearing at all. Linguistic correctness, for instance, is assumed—a paper that has not been carefully proofread is unlikely to be read at all, and thus other criteria will never be brought to bear. On the other hand, prose that E. B. White would envy, spelling and punctuation that would delight Miss Thistlebottom, lay-out and design that would thrill a medieval scribe—none of these will help a paper whose research consists of a quick glance through last month's *English Journal*. (See also the *Notes on Grading Policy in English Education Courses.*)

If, at the end of the quarter, one is unhappy with or surprised by my response to his paper, and has not conferred with me as this set of notes suggests, I'll content myself with pulling out a copy of this document and circling the appropriate passages for him. Please don't be misled by the distaste I'll probably express during the course for grades and grading, by my total distrust of numerical evaluation schemes, by my uneasiness with examinations, by my willingness in some courses to base the entire grade upon one major project, or by my inclination to allow individuals to either request or decline conferences and tests, to think that I won't grade the work, or that I won't try to apply the criteria expressed here and in *Grading Policy.*

Petulant Notes on Prose Style

I am not a master of English prose, and I won't demand that you be one, but there are certain linguistic vulgarities that do offend my sense of decency.[5] By vulgarities I don't mean the obscene and scatological—when not simply inconsequential they may well be appropriate. Rather, I mean a much more serious offense against taste. A few examples:

1. "Irregardless." Papers containing "irregardless" will not be read, irregardless of their compensating virtues.

2. "Fun" as an adjective, as in "It was a fun day." If I have reason to suspect this atrocity, I'll try to stop reading before I come to it.

---

[5] The most valuable book I've ever found on English prose is *The Elements of Style,* by William Strunk, Jr. and E. B. White (New York: The Macmillan Company, 1959 [and more recent editions]). It's small, simple, and direct, and I recommend reading it through before you begin your writing and then again when you've finished. Zinsser's book is also helpful—William Zinsser, *On Writing Well* (New York: Harper and Row, Publishers, 1976).

3. "Impact" as a verb meaning, I guess, "influence," as in "I hope our work will impact the schools." This one gives me a toothache.

4. "Which" to begin a defining relative clause. Don't use "which" when "that" is called for. "Which" does not sound more literary or formal—it simply sounds wrong, unless, of course, the clause is nondefining.

5. "The reason is because." Tell us *what* the reason is, not *why* it is.

6. "Verbal" to mean "oral," as in "Would you like that information verbally or in writing?" "Verbal" means "in, or having to do with, words." The either/or relationship in the example indicates that if the message is written, it won't be in words.

7. "Between he and I." Prepositions and transitive verbs take objects. "You should give A's to Jim and I" may be revised in either of two ways: "You should give A's to Jim and me," or "You should give F's to Jim and I."

8. "Myself" for "me," as in "They gave the papers to the chairman and myself." "Myself" is either reflexive or intensive—it should not be substituted for "me" in other circumstances.

9. "Comprise" for "compose." The whole comprises the parts; the parts compose the whole.

10. "Enthused." Presumably concocted to duplicate the function of "enthusiastic," which still does its job adequately, even enthusiastically.

11. "Typical example." Redundant—if it isn't typical, it can't be an example.

12. "Orientate" for "orient," "conferencing" for "conferring," "inferencing" for "inferring," and other such absurdities—don't make verbs out of nouns, leaving perfectly good verbs lying around with nothing to do. If you must quote something that uses a term like "conferencing," be sure to follow it with "[sic]" so that your reader will know the offense is not yours. Better yet, don't bother reading anything that indulges in such concoctions.

13. "He/she," "him or her," "s/he," and the like. They are ridiculous and unnecessary. When sex is unspecified or irrelevant, even a semiliterate reader of normal psycho-sexual maturation can figure out what the two possibilities are. (I acknowledge, bitterly, that there are some organizations, including, sadly, the National Council of Teachers of English, that actually demand these dismal phrasings.) Use the generic "he," or, if you don't like that, declare "she" to be generic and use it. Alternate back and forth between the two if you must. Sometimes, but not always, you'll be able to avoid the issue entirely by using plural forms.

14. "The present researcher," or similar pomposities. If you did something or think something, say it directly and openly and simply—"I did it," or "I think it."

15. "Less" used for "fewer." Use "fewer" with count nouns. I'd have listed fewer offenses if I'd seen less carelessness in papers. Be careful, too, with

potentially confused pairs such as "infer" and "imply," and "effect" and "affect."

16. "Self-worth," "self-identity," and the like. The "self-" indicates some action performed upon the self, as in "self-evaluation." There is no action at all indicated by "worth," much less reflexive action, and so the compound is silly, pretentious, inaccurate, and unnecessary.

17. "Literally" used to mean "figuratively." If something literally drove you up the wall, we will expect to see you perched, like a fly, somewhere near the ceiling. Of all the linguistic pretensions, this one may be the most absurd because it so loudly proclaims that the speaker doesn't know what the words mean.

18. Please limit yourself to one exclamation mark per paper—that's all the excitement I can take at the end of the quarter.

I grant that in these eighteen points I lay myself open to the charge of taking a sledge hammer to delicate stylistic tastes. I prefer to think of it as a forthright statement of personal views, which you are, of course, free to disregard as you write, though I have found them impossible to disregard as I read.

BIBLIOGRAPHY

Barzun, Jacques. *Simple and Direct: A Rhetoric for Writers.* New York: Harper and Row, Publishers, 1975.

Barzun, Jacques, and Graff, Henry F. *The Modern Researcher.* New York: Harcourt, Brace, and World, Inc., 1970.

Belanoff, Pat, et al. *The Right Handbook.* Upper Montclair, New Jersey: Boynton/Cook, 1986.

Bernstein, Theodore M. *The Careful Writer: A Modern Guide to English Usage.* New York: Atheneum, 1967.

Fowler, H. W. *A Dictionary of Modern English Usage.* London: Oxford University Press, 1926 (reprinted 1938).

Fowler, H. W., and Fowler, F. G. *The King's English.* 3rd ed. London: Oxford University Press, 1931 (reprinted 1949).

Gowers, Sir Ernest. *Plain Words: Their ABC.* New York: Alfred A. Knopf, 1968.

Strunk, William, Jr., and White, E. B. *The Elements of Style.* New York: The Macmillan Company, 1959.

Turabian, Kate L. *A Manual for Writers of Term Papers, Theses, and Dissertations,* 4th ed. Chicago: University of Chicago Press, 1973.

Zinsser, William. *On Writing Well.* New York: Harper and Row, Publishers, 1976.

Syllabus 3

Materials and Methods in English
Rutgers University
Michael W. Smith
20 Graduate School of Education
Office hours: Tues. 1:00–3:00, Wednesday 11:00–12:00
and by appointment

COURSE DESCRIPTION

This course has two primary purposes: (1) to provide an opportunity to articulate your vision of yourself as a teacher and the implications of that vision and (2) to engage you in developing instructional strategies that will help you enact that vision. I don't mean to imply that I think that all visions of teaching are equal. Through the course of the course, I'll be sharing my vision of teaching with you. I hope it's persuasive. I also hope that you'll give my vision of teaching the same sort of careful scrutiny I'll be giving yours.

COURSE REQUIREMENTS

1. I expect that everyone will come to class prepared to discuss the readings. Class participation will count for 20% of your grade. Your grade may also be lowered if you miss more than one class. I may fail you if you miss three or more classes.

In keeping with the two primary purposes of the course, you will have two primary assignments:

2. Keeping a journal of your thoughts about teaching and most importantly about the kind of teacher you want to become. Every week you must write at least two entries. Your entries should be of two kinds:

A. Reflections on your reading. Each week you should write a commentary on the reading that you've done. The commentary might include your reactions to the reading, the questions you have, the points you think are most worthy of discussion, or anything else related to the reading that you'd like to write about.

B. Reflections on teaching. Some suggestions:

1. Your metaphor for teaching. We'll be working in class to write metaphors. I'd like you to revisit your metaphor at least twice during the course of the semester.

2. Commentaries on images of teachers from popular culture. Images of teachers from television, novels, and stories often affect how we view what our job is. They certainly reflect our culture's myths about what good teaching is. At the very least, they provide common texts about teaching that will help us share our views. If you read a story or see a film that you find provocative, please share it with the class.

3. Commentaries on the stories of actual teachers. You may find these in journals or books. *Through Teachers' Eyes: Portraits of Writing Teachers at Work* is on reserve at Alexander, but you may write about any stories you choose.

4. Interviews with people about their best and worst teachers. One mistake most of us make is believing that our experience is true for everyone. The interviews should put this belief to the test. This part of the journal will be especially useful if you interview a diverse group of people.

Each week you go to your practicum placement you should also write about what you observed, what you did, and your reactions to what you observed and did. The weeks you go to your practicum, therefore, you'll have three entries.

Please date and number (e.g., week 1, number 1) all of your entries. In addition, please keep a running total of the time you've spent on your practicum assignment. You should write for at least 30 minutes on each entry.

I'll be collecting the journals from time to time and responding to them. I'll grade the journals on the basis of their thoughtfulness and the effort that went into them.

3. Develop a portfolio of lessons. This portfolio should include a prereading lesson, a prewriting lesson, a plan for the discussion of a poem, a description of a unit that includes literature and composition activities as well as a plan for evaluating students' progress, and a personal statement in which you assess your progress in becoming a teacher. I'll be commenting on your lessons as you write them. I'll schedule a conference with each of you to discuss your portfolios at which time we'll discuss what grade they should receive. Any or all of your lessons may be written in collaboration with a colleague.

Each of the major assignments will be worth 40% of your grade.

READINGS

Books and Monographs

Anson, C. (Ed.) (1989). *Writing and response.* Urbana, IL: NCTE.

Gere, A., Fairbanks, C., Howes, A., Roop, L., & Schaafsma, D. (1992). *Language and reflection: An integrated approach to teaching English.* New York: Macmillan.

Shaughnessy, M. (1977). *Errors and expectations.* New York: Oxford University Press.

Smagorinsky, P., McCann, T., & Kern, S. (1987). *Explorations: Introductory activities for literature and composition, 7–12.* Urbana, IL: ERIC.

Smith, M.W. (1991). *Understanding unreliable narrators: Reading between the lines in the literature classroom.* Urbana, IL: NCTE.

Articles

Delpit, L. (1988). The silenced dialogue: Power and pedagogy in educating other people's children. *Harvard Educational Review, 58,* 280–298.

Fine, M. Silencing in public schools. *Language Arts, 64,* 157–174.

Hillocks, G., Jr. (1986). The writer's knowledge: Theory, research, and implications for practice. In A. Petrosky and D. Bartholomae (Eds.), *The teaching of writing. 85th yearbook of the National Society for the Study of Education* (pp. 71–94). Chicago: University of Chicago Press.

Hillocks, G., Jr. (1989). Literary texts in classrooms. In P.W. Jackson & S. Haroutunian-Gordon (Eds.), *From Socrates to software: Teachers as texts and texts as teachers. 88th yearbook of the National Society for the Study of Education* (pp. 135–158). Chicago: University of Chicago Press.

Jordan, J. (1988). Nobody mean more to me than you and the future life of Willie Jordan. *Harvard Educational Review, 58,* 363–374.

Newkirk, T. (1984). Looking for trouble: A way to unmask our readings. *College English, 46,* 756–766.

Nystrand, M., & Gamoran, A. (1991). Student engagement: When recitation becomes conversation. In H. Waxman & H. Wallberg (Eds.), *Effective teaching: Current research* (pp. 257–276). Berkeley, CA: McCutchan.

Probst, R. (1992). Five kinds of literary knowing. In J. Langer (Ed.), *Literature instruction: A focus on student response* (pp. 54–77). Urbana, IL: NCTE.

Rabinowitz, P. (1991). A thousand times and never alike: Re-reading for class. A paper presented at the Midwinter Conference of the National Council of Teachers of English Assembly for Research, Chicago.

Smith, M., & Hillocks, G. (1988). Sensible sequencing: Developing knowledge about literature text by text. *English Journal, 78*(2), 58–63.

SCHEDULE

A Vision of Ourselves as Teachers

9/1:   An introduction to the course and to each other.
Thinking about our goals and how to achieve them.
Assignment: Read Gere et al., chapters 4–5.

9/8:   Perspective on teaching English I.
Assignment: Read Gere et al., chapters 6–8.

9/15:   Perspectives on teaching English II.
Assignment: Read Gere et al., chapters 2–3. Read Delpit, Fine, Jordan. Write your metaphor for teaching.

9/22:   Thinking about difference.
Sharing our metaphors.
Assignment: Read Hillocks "The writer's knowledge."

Considering Composition

9/29:   What knowledge do students need before they write.
          Thinking about the research paper.
          Assignment: Write a prewriting lesson.

10/6:   Sharing lessons.
          Assignment: Read Chapters 11, 15 and 16 in Anson.

10/13:   Responding to writing: Theory into Practice.
          Assignment: Read Chapters 3–4 in Shaughnessy.

10/20:   Considering correctness.
          Putting it all together: How will you teach writing.
          Assignment: Read Probst.

Looking at Literature

10/27:   Thinking about our goals.
          What do we want students to bring to texts: An analysis of think
              aloud protocols.
          Assignment: Read Smagorinsky et al.

11/3:   Introductory activities.
          Assignment: Write an introductory activity. Read Smith & Hillocks.
              Read Smith.

11/10:   Sharing activities.
          Developing units of literature.
          Assignment: Read Hillocks "Literary texts in classrooms" and
              Nystrand and Gamoran.

11/17:   Talking about literature.
          Assignment: Develop plan for a discussion of a short poem. Read
              Newkirk and Rabinowitz.

12/1:   Sharing discussion plans.
          Sharing ourselves as readers.
          Assignment: Read Gere et al., Chapter 9.

12/8   Thinking about evaluation.
          Exam day: Reprise.

Syllabus 4

SPRING, 1994

ENGLISH 485
Problems in Teaching Composition, Language,
Literature and Reading in High School

T & Th Faner 2363, 11:00 a.m. to 12:15 p.m.

Bruce C. Appleby
Professor of English
Professor of Curriculum and Instruction
Office: Faner 2221
Hours: 1:30 to 3:00 p.m. T & Th and by appointment

TEXTS

Coursepack at Kopies and More

Proett & Gill, *The Writing Process in Action,* NCTE, 1986. Purchase at University Book Store

Student Membership in National Council of Teachers of English, for which you will receive the *English Journal*

"... (there are) five ways in which the English methods course can make a unique contribution which justifies its being absolutely necessary:

1. organization of and drawing together of the components of the discipline; 2. necessity and means of skills instruction; 3. communication with and understanding of the world of the adolescent; 4. development of a reasonable perspective toward [the student's] own high school training; and 5. development of an attitude and enthusiasm toward English teaching."

Appleby, Bruce C. "Is a Methods Course Necessary? On What Grounds?" in *Method in the Teaching of English*, Stryker, ed. NCTE, 1967.

GOALS

Given the above description of what a methods course should be, we'll spend the semester looking at the current situation in junior and senior high school English, discuss the teacher's role in all this, and look at how English is and can be taught. Throughout the semester, remember that I feel the course should be more aptly titled Methods of *Learning* English, since that is where the emphasis will be.

ACTIVITIES

Each class member should plan to participate actively in the class discussions and to prepare and present materials to the class. The reading list highlights the major topics we will look at: The Adolescent Today — Teaching and Learning: Are They Compatible? — Language — Writing — Reading and Literature. We will discuss the materials as assigned and work with the methods we would use in teaching the ideas. Throughout, I intend that the class activities will exemplify various teaching methods.

READING/RESPONSE JOURNALS

There are two purposes for the journal you will keep for ENGL 485. The first and most important is to provide a place for you to react to the readings. The second is to provide a place for you to respond to various teaching practices and classroom activities. I want you to find personal connections to the reading and for you to think about, learn, and understand course materials.

I expect each entry to have a purpose. There are no length restrictions, but I do predict you will end up writing about five pages a week. Label each entry (title of what is being responded to, date, etc.). Proofreading is a courtesy because I need to be able to make sense of what you write. I will NOT expect polished prose or completely thought-out ideas. Journals are writing-in-progress. You will NEVER be graded on journals as if the entries were finished papers.

A reading/response journal records summaries of, reactions to, and comparisons of like or conflicting views of assigned readings. Find the central idea. Wonder. Question. REACT to the text you've read. You may wish to keep your class notes in the journal. If so, be sure to make it clear to me what is a note you've taken and what is a response to that note.

I will collect and read your journals three or four times during the semester. I will NOT give your journal a letter grade when I read it. I will record how much you wrote and I will respond as I read. At the end of the semester, I will give your journal a point grade based on amount of writing and quality of the entries in terms of focus, purpose, thought, and thinking effort reflected. Again, I will NOT grade on grammar, spelling, punctuation, mechanics, usage or any of those other technical aspects English teachers so stereotypically get involved with.

ASSIGNMENTS, ATTENDANCE, AND GRADES

Assignments are due at the beginning of class on the day for which they are assigned. Discussions and class activities will be built around the supposition that you have read the material assigned and come to class with questions and reactions. *If my supposition is proven incorrect by nonparticipation, you are inviting me to please give you quizzes over the reading.*

I expect you to be here and on time for each class meeting. There is no policy of "permitted number of cuts." Being in class to receive or do an assignment or an in-class activity is your responsibility. If you are going to be absent, I expect you to clear the absence with me before it occurs.

Grades will be based on ungraded reading and reaction assignments (not to do an assignment is to choose to receive a grade of F), journals, approximately six written projects, a "term paper" which will be a teaching unit you will prepare, and class participation. You will be doing lessons plans and papers of varying length and complexity. (To give you an idea of how I grade, I have had 100 students in this class the last five times I have taught it. Grades were: A = 31; B = 36; C = 24; D = 3; F = 6.)

READINGS AND UNITS OF STUDY

Most of these are in your coursepack. Some will be photocopied material I will be handing out and still others will be dittoes I have on hand, made *before* the recent changes in copyright laws. In addition, there will be for each unit extensive bibliographies I've prepared, such as "A Somewhat Ideal Bibliography of Necessary Books in English Education," "A Bibliography of PRO-Grammar Articles," "A Bibliography of How to Teach Language, Not Just Grammar," etc. (*EJ* refers to the *English Journal; CE* to *College English; LA* to *Language Arts;* and *CCC* to *College Composition and Communication*).

The Adolescent Today

Making the Best of Adolescence
(from Atwell *In the Middle: Writing, Reading and Learning with Adolescents* Boynton/Cook-Heinemann, 1987, 24–50)
Memo to Student Teachers
(Lazarski, *EJ*, V. 76, # 5, Sep., 1987, 93–94)
Dear Professor: This Is What I Want You to Know
(Workman, *Phi Delta Kappan*, May, 1986, 668–671)
Basic Rules of Teenage Life
(Pfeffer, *ALAN Review*, V. 17, # 3, Spring, 1990, 5–7)
Finding Out About Your Students
(from Appleby & Purves, *Journeys, Responding* series, Ginn, 1973, T-55–T-64)

Teaching and Learning: Are They Compatible?

How Children Learn or How Teachers Teach?
(Lindfors, *LA*, V. 61, # 6, Oct., 1984, 600–606)
Thinking and English Classes
(Barwick, *CE*, V. 43, # 2, Feb., 1981, 179–188)
How Do We Teach?
(Carlsen, *EJ*, V. 54, # 5, May, 1965, 364–368)
Tasting Failure: Thoughts of an At-Risk Learner
(Hill, *Phi Delta Kappan*, V. 73, # 4, Dec., 1991, 308–310)
Collaborative Learning and Teaching Writing: What We Know and Need to Know about Peer-Response Groups
(Fox, SLATE Starter Sheet, March, 1993)
The Teacher as Mid-Wife
(Belenky et al., *Women's Ways of Knowing*, Basic Books, 1986)

Language

Language Acquisition and the Teaching and Learning of Writing
(Falk, *CE*, V. 41, # 4, Dec., 1979, 436–447)
The Uses of Grammar
(from Weaver *Grammar for Teachers*, NCTE, 1979, 3–6)
Grammar, Grammars and the Teaching of Grammar
(Hartwell, *CE*, V. 47, # 2, Feb., 1985, 105–127)

Forward to the Basics: Getting Down to Grammar
        (DeBeaugrande, *CCC*, V. 35, # ?, ?, 1984, 358–367)
Grammar in Context: Why and How
        (Meyer, Youga, & Flint-Ferguson, *EJ*, V. 79, # 1, Jan., 1990, 66–70)
Not All Errors Are Created Equal: Nonacademic Readers in the Professions
Respond to Lapses in Usage
        (Hairston, *CE*, V. 43, # 8, Dec., 1981, 794–806)
Explaining Grammatical Concepts
        (Harris & Rowan, *Journal of Basic Writing*, V. 8, # 2, 1989, 21–41)
It Bees Dat Way Sometime
        (from Smitherman, *Talkin' and Testifyin': The Language of Black America*,
        Houghton-Mifflin, 1987, 16–34)
Standard Academic English and My Kentucky Dialect
        (Broaddus, *Advanced Composition Forum*, V. 4, # 1, 1993, 1–3)
Literate Traditions
        (from Heath, *Ways with Words*, Cambridge University Press, 1983, 190–
        235)

Writing

Reading/Writing Workshops
        (Atwell, *American Educator*, Spring, 1989)
Writing: An Act of Cognition
        (Fulwiler, from Griffin, ed., *New Directions in the Teaching of Writing*,
        Jossey-Bass, 1982, 15–25)
The Experiential Approach: Inner Worlds to Outer
        (Judy, in Donovan & McClellands, eds., *Eight Approaches in Teaching Com-
        position*, NCTE, 1980, 37–52)
Composition Course: Pursuit of Ideas
        (Pierce, in Myers & Gray, eds., *Theory and Practice in the Teaching of Com-
        position*, NCTE, 1983, 144–149)
The Writing Assignment: An Obstacle or a Vehicle?
        (Jenkins, *EJ*, V. 69, # 9, Dec., 1980, 66–69)
But It's Just My Opinion
        (Miller, in Sudol, ed., *Revising: New Essays for Teachers of Writing*, NCTE,
        1982)
Nonjudgmental Responses to Students' Writing
        (Johnston, *EJ*, V. 71, # 4, April, 1982, 50–53)
Developing Correctness in Student Writing: Alternatives to the Error Hunt
        (Rosen, *EJ*, V. 76, # 3, March, 1987, 62–69)
Minimal Marking
        (Haswell, *CE*, V. 45, # 6, Oct., 1983, 600–604)
Using Reading in the Writing Classroom
        (Qualley, in Newkirk, ed., *Nuts and Bolts: A Practical Guide to Teaching
        College Composition*, Heinemann, 1993, 101–127)

Reading and Literature

A set of reviews of four high school literature anthologies

(Appleby, Johnson & Taylor, *EJ*, V. 78, # 6, Oct., 1989; V. 79, # 4, April, 1990; V. 79, # 6, Oct., 1990; V. 80, # 7, Nov, 1991, ?)
Literature Anthologies in the U.S.: Impediments to Good Teaching Practice
    (Zaharias, *EJ*, V. 78, # 6, Oct., 1989, 22–27)
Expanding the Secondary Literature Program: Annotated Bibliographies of American Indian, Asian American, and Hispanic American Literature
    (Duff & Tongchinsub, *English Education*, V. 22, # 4, Dec., 1990, 220–240)
The Act of Reading
    (Early & Ericson, in Nelms, ed., *Literature in the Classroom*, NCTE, 1988, 31–44)
Readers and Literary Texts
    (Probst, in Nelms, see above, 19–29)
Re-creating the Literary Text: Practice and Theory
    (Greco, *EJ*, V. 79, # 7, Nov., 1990, 34–40)
Adolescent Literature and the English Curriculum
    (Probst, *EJ*, V. 76, # 3, March, 1987, 26–30)
None of Us Is Smarter Than All of Us: The Reform in California's Curriculum
    (Taylor, *EJ*, V. 77, # 8, Dec., 1988, ?)
Report from the Institute: Notes on the Teaching of Literature
    (Gruenberg, *EJ*, V. 75, # 6, Oct., 1986, 30–32)
Twenty (Better) Questions
    (Myers, K., *EJ*, V. 77, # 1, Jan., 1988, 64–65)
Literature Study Groups: Teachers, Texts and Readers
    (Rabin, *EJ*, V. 79, # 7, Nov., 1990, 41–46)
Reading, Writing, and Talking: Using Literature Study Groups
    (Gille, *EJ*, V. 78, # 1, Jan., 1989,?)
Seventh Graders Sharing Literature: How Did We Get Here?
    (Close, *LA*, V. 67, # ?, Dec., 1990, ?)

Syllabus 5

English 481
The Teaching of English
317 Lincoln Hall
12:30-1:45 PM, Tues. & Thurs.

"It's a slow transition," said Dr. Joseph DeRose Jr., speaking of the process by which young medical doctors become full-fledged members of their profession. "The first year you see everything as the patient would and only gradually get indoctrinated into the fraternity of medicine. But by the end you really have adopted the physician's view of things. It's a shame we can't hang on to the earlier attitude, though. I think we would all be better doctors if we could."
Quoted in *The New York Times*, Sunday, 11/28/93, Sec. 4, p. 4

COURSE DESCRIPTION

Two aims shape my approach to English 481. First, I want to help you to understand and become fluent in the prevailing literacy practices of your chosen profession—secondary English education. Second, I wish to encourage you to question these literacy practices and to consider how you might change them, given your knowledge of other literacy practices such as those exercised by young adults and progressive English educators. My overarching goal is to prepare you to become a participant in the conversations of an English education "fraternity" without losing sight of the fact that this fraternity (like any institutionalized community) is sometimes quite rigid and narrow-minded in its thinking.

What do I mean by the phrase "literacy practices"? I mean all those acts of reading, writing, and speaking that secondary English teachers enact in the course of their working lives. For instance, many high school teachers, like myself here, write syllabi for the courses they are responsible for teaching. Other literacy practices include the leading of a discussion; the reading of Young Adult literature; the presentation of mini-lessons; the writing of comments on student papers; and the organization of group projects. The list goes on and on. In any case, there are numerous reading, writing, and speaking practices which exemplary teachers of high school English engage in at one time or another. I can't promise that I will prepare you for all of the practices you will find yourself enacting as a student teacher and in the years to come (for instance, I'm not sure I can or want to help you to learn how to bellow like a impatient cook in a crowded mess hall when students move too slowly from the school corridors into your classroom), but I do hope to cover a broad range of activities that you will certainly find yourself involved in as a beginning teacher.

These are some of the literacy practices that I anticipate all of us will undertake at one point or another this semester:

— research biographical, literary, and historical information important for teaching conventional high school reading materials

— present information in 10–15 minute mini-lessons

— write lesson plans covering an extended period of time (about two weeks)

— create interesting and student-centered group projects

— evaluate one's own oral and written acts of communication

— evaluate others' acts of oral and written communication

— read fiction for young adults

— write fiction for young adults

— research the literacy interests of young adults

— organize and partake in computer conferences

— acquire multicultural resources

— videotape one's teaching performance

— share and present papers in a professional setting

— create good questions for discussion

— draw pictures

— role-play and improvise

— sing songs

— express coherently one's approach to the teaching of English

This list doesn't quite cover everything we will do; I expect to improvise as we go along, and I want to include those literacy practices that I haven't thought of but that you think you need to learn more about in order to be an effective high school English teacher. When you finish reading this course description and the enclosed syllabus and statement on evaluation and assessment, I want you to make a list of other activities and/or concerns that you would like me and/or others to address before the end of this semester. On Thursday, I will ask you to share your ideas with me and we can adjust the enclosed syllabus accordingly. I ask you to do this because I want to broaden my own understanding of what prospective teachers feel they need to learn before they begin teaching, and because I want to make sure that the activities we engage in this semester are useful to you.

Over the years, I have found the literacy practice in which I am engaged here quite important for creating an environment where learning can occur. In my experience, good teachers indicate to their students, either in writing or in oral discourse, their goals and objectives. Studies like that conducted by Mihaly Csikszentmihalyi and his colleagues (the results of which are recorded in *Talented Teens: The Roots of Success and Failure,* a book we will read excerpts from later in the semester) suggest that optimal learning occurs when students perceive clear goals and receive immediate and unambiguous feedback on their attempts to achieve those goals (14). I share their perspective, and I think the same might be said for teachers: when we understand the goals and objectives of our students, and when we get feedback on our attempts to meet those goals and objectives, we are likely to create an optimal learning situation. In this class, I will consult with you as we go along to make sure that my aims are clearly understood and meeting your needs; conversely, as the semester moves along, I will give you feedback as you draft goals and objectives for your own teaching, and as you engage in the various literacy practices that typify the work of secondary English teachers.

I'm not sure how to characterize my approach to this class in secondary English education. I know that I don't conceive English 481 as a class in whole language pedagogy, nor do I think of it as a class in feminist or radical pedagogy—although I am drawn to the student-centered and dialogic nature of these three theoretical frameworks. I don't think of this course as a class devoted to a "back-to-the-basics" or "skills-based" approach to learning, although I do recognize that in some sense I am suggesting that there are core practices that demarcate the teaching of English. And, even though I anticipate that we will swap war stories about teaching and borrow lesson plans from one another, I certainly don't conceive this class as a place where ideas are shared without reflection.

Ultimately, I think what I am trying to do in this class is to create a context where people can talk reasonably and passionately to one another despite the fact that they have different assumptions about how to teach English. In my experience, prospective teachers have quite different and conflicting viewpoints about the best way to educate adolescents; furthermore, prospective teachers often possess allegiances to more than one "theory" of teaching (just like experienced teachers). My goal is not so much to teach a single approach to the teaching of English as to create a context where different approaches can be explored and debated. I hope that by the end of the semester we will feel comfortable exploring our differences because we have acknowledged and discussed our commonalities (such as the fact that all of us, at one time or another, will have to present mini-lessons to our students). I hope to participate in a classroom where viewpoints can be exchanged, and even changed, without fear of intimidation or reprisal.

I'm not sure what to call this kind of classroom. I know that I like to think that my pedagogy centers upon inquiry and problem-posing. The terms "democratic education" and "community-building" are appealing to me, too. Maybe by the end of the term, as I read and write with you, I will come to a better way of situating my own approach to the teaching of English.

In the two enclosed handouts, you will find more specific information that ought to be helpful to you as you attempt to get a better sense of this class and my own approach to the teaching of English. The first document I hope you will look at is the syllabus. This syllabus is fairly detailed for the first six weeks and then gets a bit more general. I might have to pass out another syllabus at a later date in the semester, especially if there are a number of concerns that people want me to incorporate into the class. The second document is a statement on evaluation and assessment. In this text, I state my approach to evaluation and I describe the portfolios that I will assess. As I mentioned, at our next meeting, I'll look to answer your questions and I'll anticipate receiving some suggestions for change.

Finally, here is some important information you need to know. I'll use a form that I hope is easy to read and readily accessible.

Name: Thomas Philion (Tom)
Office: 1902 University Hall
Phone: ——— (o), ——— (h)
Office Hours: 10:00–12:00 T, Th

Note: One conference with me before Spring Break is required of all participants in this class. I will be happy to meet outside of office hours where there are conflicts.

Required Texts: *In The Middle*, by Nancie Atwell

Language and Reflection, by Anne Gere, et al.

Coursepack

Some copying of texts for distribution to the class will be required.

Suggested Texts: *The First Year of Teaching*
How Porcupines Make Love II

General Principles Regarding Attendance: Attendance and promptness are expected. More than three missed classes and a failure to turn in written work on time can only negatively influence your grade. If you fall behind in your work, you need to see me immediately. I will give out incompletes only in exceptional circumstances.

UNIT ONE: AN INTRODUCTION TO THE LITERACY PRACTICES OF SECONDARY ENGLISH TEACHERS

Jan. 11: Distribution of Syllabus, Course Description; Introductions. Description of Different Research Possibilities for Portfolio One (*Beowulf, The Canterbury Tales, Romeo and Juliet*, works by Edgar Allan Poe, *Of Mice and Men, Lord of the Flies, The Crucible*, or *To Kill A Mockingbird*).
  Homework: Read "The Teaching of Literature in Illinois Schools," by Teresa Faulkner. Find Copies of the text(s) you have selected.

Jan. 13: Discuss article and form small groups.
  Homework: Gather relevant historical, biographical, literary, and pedagogical information regarding your text(s).

Jan. 18: Discuss characteristics of a good presentation; meet in small groups and organize activities.

Jan. 20: Small-group presentations. Distribute annotated bibliographies.
  Homework: Read articles in coursepack on engaging students in reading and writing. Highlight ideas which interest you and ideas about which you have questions.

Jan. 25: Small-group presentations. Distribute annotated bibliographies.

Jan. 27: Discuss how to engage students in learning and group projects.
  Homework: Create a two-week unit plan.

Feb. 1: Brainstorm qualities of good lesson plans. Share ideas. Distribute copies of unit plan to small-group members and to Tom.
  Homework: Write a critical response to the unit plans you receive from small-group members.

Feb. 3: Share responses to unit plans in small groups; give copies of your responses to Tom; discuss issues that are emerging in small groups.
  Homework: Revise unit plans.

Feb. 8: Small-group modeling of an assignment; issue discussion.

Feb. 10: Small-group modeling of an assignment; issue discussion.
  Homework: Read Chapters 1 and 2 of *In The Middle* and write a journal entry. Prepare Portfolio One.

Feb. 15: Portfolio One due; Introduction to Portfolio Two.
    Homework: Create discussion questions for Thursday.

UNIT TWO: STUDENT-CENTERED APPROACHES
TO THE TEACHING OF ENGLISH

Feb: 17: Turn in Journal Entry on *In The Middle;* Discuss first two chapters.
    Homework: Read Section Two, "Writing Workshop," in *In The Middle,* and write a journal response.

Feb. 22: Writing Workshop: Benjamin Warr
    Homework: Reconsider your journal response in light of our writing workshop. Create discussion questions for Thursday.

Feb. 24: Turn in Journal Entries; Discuss Section Two of *In The Middle.*
    Homework: Read Section Three of *In The Middle* and write a journal response.

March 1: Presentation by Jane Bysack, Young Adult Librarian at Oak Park Public Library.
    Homework: Reconsider your response to Section Three in light of our presentation.

March 3: Turn in journal entries; Discuss Section Three of *In The Middle* and implications of Atwell's approach for our own teaching.

March 8: NO CLASS: SPRING BREAK!!
March 10:

March 15: Writing Workshop (what makes a good story?); Distribute draft copies of story to peers and to Tom.
    Homework: Write a critical response to stories.

March 17: Share responses. Presentation on publishing student writing.
    Homework: Revise stories.

March 22: Introduction to Scailab and computer-mediated teaching. Computer-mediated conference on reading surveys and how to integrate young adult literature into English curriculums.

March 24: Share revised stories and meet in peer conferences.
    Homework: Prepare Portfolio Two.

March 29: Portfolio Two due; Guest presentation by Ginger Brent, English teacher at North Shore Country Day School.

March 31: Presentation on acquiring resources in multicultural literature.
    Homework: Read Chapters 1–4 in *Language and Reflection.*

UNIT THREE: HOW SHOULD WE APPROACH THE TEACHING OF ENGLISH?

April 5: Brainstorm metaphors for our approach to teaching.

April 7: Response Papers: Language as Artifact.

April 12: Response Papers: Language as Development.

April 14: Response Papers: Language as Expression.

April 19: Response Papers: Language as Social Construct.

April 21: Discussion: Issues in Classroom Management.
   Homework: Read Chapters 8-10 in *Language and Reflection.*

April 26: Roundtable discussion with Student Teachers, University Supervisors, and Cooperating Teachers.

April 28: Class Wrap-Up and Evaluation.

May 2: Portfolio Three Due.

STATEMENT ON EVALUATION AND ASSESSMENT

Recently, the term "portfolio" has become quite popular in texts dealing with writing instruction. Some of you no doubt have heard the term used by teachers and some of you might even have prepared a portfolio at some point in your academic careers. As you might expect with a term so suddenly popular, people mean different things when they use this term. Some people use the term to describe a collection of all the writing (rough drafts, notes, finished pieces, revisions, etc.) that was completed by a student during a certain period of time. Others use the term to describe a collection of "finished" pieces that a student has selected and self-evaluated. Still others use the term to describe a collection of graded and ungraded writing which will ultimately be re-evaluated by an instructor.

In any case, the term portfolio refers to a folder that holds a collection of writing—just as in art classes the term "portfolio" refers to a folder or some other contraption in which one collects pieces of artistic work. Those of you who are interested in learning more about the written scholarship on portfolios should consult Chapter 9 of *Language and Reflection.*

In this class, I will use portfolios to evaluate your growth and proficiency with respect to some of the literacy practices that I listed in the course description. By "growth," I mean your ability to revise and alter your thinking as you engage in conversations about those literacy practices with myself and your peers. By "proficiency," I mean your ability to translate into action our talk about what makes a particular practice of writing or speaking "exemplary." Some people use the terms "effort" and "quality" to describe what I refer to here. Others use the terms "process" and "product." In any case, in any one portfolio, I ultimately will assess both your "growth" as a writer/speaker and your "proficiency" with respect to certain kinds of literacy practices.

I will ask you to submit three portfolios during the course of the semester. Each portfolio should be turned in to me at the end of each unit that I outlined in the syllabus. Each of the units focuses on related literacy practices. For instance, in unit one, I ask you to research background information regarding a conventional high school text, to present information about that text, and to construct a unit plan that will engage high school students in an activity or project that fosters critical thinking. In unit two, I ask you to read two examples of Young Adult literature, to research the literacy practices of young adults, and to write your own story. Finally, in unit three, I ask you to write a response to a chapter in *Language and Reflection* and then to use this response to shape a statement of teaching philosophy as well as a research question to be explored during student teaching. As you can see, using a portfolio approach to evaluation enables me to link a number of different but related activities—a real improvement, from my perspective, upon a "traditional" form of evaluation which looks only at isolated and discrete literacy practices.

In most instances, we will create together the criteria that I will use to evaluate your work. For instance, before your presentation to your classmates in Unit One, you and I will brainstorm the characteristics of a good mini-lesson. When everyone has done a presentation, we will see if we can add any other criteria to our list. Similarly, as we write a unit plan, we will talk about the features of a good set of lesson plans. The same goes for the project involving the writing of fiction. When I evaluate your portfolios, I will use the criteria we develop to evaluate your work.

Additionally, I will ask you to evaluate your own work. At the end of each portfolio I will ask you to write a reflective conclusion. In this conclusion, you can share with me your own sense of what you learned, what you accomplished, and what you still need to work on. When each portfolio is turned in, I'll also ask you to give me an evaluation of my own growth and performance as an English teacher.

The grade I give you for each portfolio will be holistic in nature. In other words, I will assess your portfolio as a whole. In the past I have given one grade, but this semester I am thinking about giving two grades, one for "proficiency" and one for "growth." Let's plan to talk about this idea when the appropriate time comes.

Anyway, here is a description of what I would like to see included in each of the three portfolios that I will request of you.

Portfolio 1 is due on February 15th and should include:

(1) An introduction.

(2) An annotated and collaboratively produced bibliography of resources related to a particular literary text commonly taught in high schools (including historical, biographical, literary, and pedagogical references).

(3) Notes/text used to prepare for class presentation (if used).

(4) A self-evaluation of one's own class presentation, written after viewing a video-tape of that presentation.

(5) A set of lesson plans covering two weeks, with draft copies and critical responses from peers.

(6) A reflective conclusion.

In general, the introduction to the portfolio can be conceived as a letter to me. I find that I read the portfolios better if I get some sort of welcome to your work. You might list for me the contents of your portfolio and perhaps prepare me to focus on certain ideas or aspects of your writing before I actually read.

At some point before you get to work on your portfolios, I'll share with you models of work done by other people. For instance, on Thursday, I'll share with you two models of the annotated bibliography, and later in the term I will share models of long-term unit plans. As much as I can, I'll provide you with visual aids to help you shape your own approach to these portfolio assignments.

Portfolio 2 is due on March 29th and should consist of the following:

(1) An introduction.

(2) A reading survey (see *In The Middle*, Appendix F) which you have designed, passed out to secondary school students, and recorded the results from (and/or interview booksellers or librarians).

(3) Summaries of two different young adult novels read during the semester.

(4) A creative piece of writing in which you explore the dimensions of the genre of young adult literature that interests you. For example, if you read a horror story by Christopher Pike, you might write your own horror story. As in the first portfolio, you should include at least one draft of your story and written feedback from at least two peers.

(5) A reflective conclusion.

Portfolio 3 is due on May 2nd. It should consist of the following:

(1) An introduction.

(2) A copy of the response paper that you shared with our class in a discussion of *Language and Reflection*.

(3) A paper which either explores or states the nature of your teaching philosophy.

(4) A prospectus for a teacher-research project to be completed during your semester of student teaching.

(5) A reflective conclusion.

Again, as we go along, I will fill in gaps and provide information where it is necessary. I'll look forward to your questions on Thursday and anticipate making alterations that you think are needed.

Appendix B: Colleges and Universities Contributing Syllabi

Arizona State University

Armstrong State College (GA)

Athens State College (AL)

Augusta College (GA)

Ball State University (IN)

Bluefield State College (WVA)

California State University–Fresno

California State University–Long Beach

California State University–Northridge

Central Michigan University

College of William and Mary (VA)

East Central College (MO)

East Central University (OK)

Emporia State University (KS)

Fairmont State College (WV)

Florida State University

Fort Hays State University (KS)

Georgia State University

Grand Valley State University (MI)

Indiana University of Pennsylvania

James Madison University (VA)

Jersey City State College (NJ)

Kansas State University

Lamar University

Langston University (OK)

Lewis-Clark State College (ID)

Moorehead State University (MN)

Morehead State University (KY)

North Carolina State University

North Dakota State University

Ohio State University

Oklahoma State University

Pembroke State University (NC)

Pennsylvania State University–Harrisburg

Peru State College (NE)

Pittsburg State University (KS)

Plymouth State College (NH)

Rhode Island College

Salem State College (MA)

Sam Houston State University (TX)

Shepherd College (WV)

Southern Arkansas University

Southern Illinois University

Southern Oregon State College

Southwest Texas State University

State University of New York–Oneonta

Towson State University (MD)

Troy State Universtiy (AL)

Virginia Commonwealth University

University of Alabama–Birmingham

University of Arizona

University of Central Florida

University of Illinois–Chicago

University of Illinois–Urbana/Champaign

University of Iowa

University of Kansas

University of Maryland–College Park

University of Massachusetts–Boston

University of Michigan–Ann Arbor

University of Michigan–Flint

University of Minnesota–Duluth

University of Nebraska–Lincoln

University of Nebraska–Omaha

University of Nevada–Las Vegas

University of Nevada–Reno

University of New Hampshire

University of North Dakota

University of Oklahoma

University of South Alabama

University of South Florida

University of Wisconsin–Eau Claire

University of Wisconsin–Madison

University of Wyoming

Washington State University

Wayne State College (NE)

West Liberty State College (WV)

Western Carolina University (NC)

Western Illinois University

Western Michigan University

Western Oregon State College

Western State College (CO)

Appendix C: Survey of Teachers of Methods Courses

As we read through the syllabi we often wondered about the experiences of the professors who were teaching the courses. Were they grizzled veterans of secondary classrooms bringing a font of practical wisdom to the nurturing of the next generation of teachers? Were they teaching assistants who had never taught a secondary school class? Did they teach in an English or education department? Were they teaching the course because they wanted to, or because they'd been stuck with the assignment? In order to get some answers to these questions, we mailed out a survey to each professor who had sent us a syllabus. The questions we asked, and the frequency of response in each category (within parentheses), are listed next.

Survey Results

1. I taught English/language arts in a secondary school for:

a. 0 years (5)

b. 1–5 years (19)

c. 5–10 years (15)

d. over 10 years (9)

2. I most recently taught English/language arts in a secondary school:

a. 0–5 years ago (14)

b. 6–10 years ago (10)

c. 11–15 years ago (6)

d. over 15 years ago (18)

3. I have taught the English/language arts teaching methods course at a university for:

a. 1–5 years (21)

b. 6–10 years (12)

c. 11–15 years (4)

d. over 15 years (11)

4. I teach the English/language arts teaching methods course:

a. because I want to (47)

b. because I am assigned to (1)

c. other (0)

5. My rank at my university is:

a. teaching assistant or instructor (1)

b. adjunct professor (0)

c. assistant professor (13)

d. associate professor (16)

e. full professor (18)

6. My appointment is in the following department:

a. English (31)

b. Curriculum and Instruction (or similar department) (15)

c. Humanities (0)

d. General Education (2)

e. other (0)

In that we did not receive a high percentage of surveys from the professors who taught the courses (forty-eight out of eighty-one responded), we need to be cautious in drawing conclusions; ergo the reporting of the survey results in an appendix rather than the body of the report. The most encouraging finding from the survey, for instance, is that all but one respondent reported teaching the methods course by choice rather than assignment. (A number of professors circled both choice and assignment, but our purpose was to see if teachers were teaching the course with enthusiasm, so we counted all double selections as "choice.") One possible conclusion from this positive news is that only professors who teach the methods course by choice are likely to return surveys giving information about their teaching experience and predilictions. We should point out that the only professor who indicated that he taught by assignment and not by choice is a good personal friend who is a distinguished scholar and legendary for his commitment to his profession; we are confident that his work with preservice teachers rivals that of anyone in the sample.

We report the survey results, then, with reservations about what they really reveal. Of those who responded, we are encouraged to see that almost all have had experience in a secondary classroom. A few full professors reported that they had taught secondary English classes within the past five years, one by choice as a way to stay in touch with schools and students, and those in California by law (*without financial compensation,* as one stressed in the margin of the syllabus). We admire and appreciate efforts by university professors to stay in touch with the realities of public school teaching. Most of us are out in schools in one way or another, supervising teachers, conducting research, doing in-services, and maintaining our contacts. Taking the time away from the responsibilities of university teaching, service, and scholarship to teach public school classes is a great commitment, one that we think professors should consider from time to time as the years spread out between their careers in the public schools and their years in the ivory tower.

We were encouraged to see as well that among those in the sample, almost all methods courses were taught by full-time faculty, rather than being staffed by adjuncts or teaching assistants. We do not wish to disparage the work of adjuncts and TAs, upon whom most universities depend greatly for many needs. Yet students come to universities to gain expertise from the full-time faculty who presumably are involved in scholarship and therefore have the greatest virtuosity in teaching the course. We all know of glaring exceptions to this rule, yet we can assume that most students would prefer to take courses from tenured and tenure-track faculty than from temporary professors.

The survey gives a rough, and possibly deceptive, idea of the characteristics of professors of secondary English methods courses. We hope that the most encouraging findings—that professors teach the courses because they want to, and that they have for the most part had experience as public school teachers—are representative of the field as a whole.

Works Cited

Anson, C.M., & Forsberg, L.L. (1990). Moving beyond the academic community: Transitional stages in professional writing. *Written Communication, 7*(2), 200–231.

Applebee, A.N. (1974). *Tradition and reform in the teaching of English: A History.* Urbana, IL: National Council of Teachers of English.

Applebee, A.N. (1986). Problems in process approaches: Toward a re–conceptualization of process instruction. In A.R. Petrosky & D. Bartholomae (Eds.), *The teaching of writing. 85th Yearbook for the National Society for the Study of Education* (pp. 95–113). Chicago: University of Chicago Press.

Applebee, A.N. (1993). *Literature in the secondary school: Studies of curriculum and instruction in the United States.* NCTE Research Report No. 25. Urbana, IL: National Council of Teachers of English.

Atwell, N. (1987). *In the middle: Writing, reading, and learning with adolescents.* Upper Montclair, NJ: Boynton/Cook.

Beach, R. (1993). *A teacher's introduction to reader-response theories.* Urbana, IL: National Council of Teachers of English.

Beach, R., & Marshall, J. (1991). *Teaching literature in the secondary school.* San Diego: Harcourt, Brace, Jovanovich.

Borko, H. (1985). Student teachers' planning and evaluations of reading lessons. In J. Niles & R. Lalik (Eds.), *Issues in literacy: A research perspective. 34th yearbook of the National Reading Conference* (pp. 57–72). New York: National Reading Conference.

Borko, H. (1989). Research on learning to teach: Implications for graduate teacher preparation. In A.E. Woolfolk (Ed.), *Research perspectives on the graduate preparation of teachers* (pp. 69–87). Englewood Cliffs, NJ: Prentice-Hall.

Borko, H., Lalik, R., Livingston, C., Pecic, K., & Perry, D. (1986). Learning to teach in the induction year: Two case studies. Paper presented at the annual meeting of the American Educational Research Association, San Francisco. April.

Borko, H., Lalik, R., & Tomchin, E. (1987). Student teachers' understandings of successful teaching. *Teaching and Teacher Education, 3,* 77–90.

Britton, J., Burgess, T., Martin, N., McLeod, A., & Rosen, H. (1975). *The development of writing abilities (11–18).* London: Macmillan Education Ltd. for the Schools Council.

Brooks, C., Jr., & Warren, R.P. (1938). *Understanding poetry: An anthology for college students.* New York: Henry Holt.

Brown, J.S., Collins, A., & Duguid, P. (1989). Situated cognition and the culture of learning. *Educational Researcher, 18,* 32–42.

Bruner, J. S. (1975). From communication to language: A psychological perspective. *Cognition, 3,* 255–287.

Cazden, C.B. (1988). *Classroom discourse: The language of teaching and learning.* Portsmouth, NH: Boynton/Cook-Heinemann.

Clark, V.P., Eschholz, P.A., & Rosen, A.F. (Eds.). (1985). *Language: Introductory readings.* New York: St. Martin's.

Csikszentmihalyi, M. (1982). Learning, "flow," and happiness. In R. Gross (Ed.), *Invitation to life-long learning* (pp. 166–187). Chicago: Follett Publishing.

Farb, P. (1981). *Word play: What happens when.* New York: Knopf.

Feiman-Nemser, S. (1983). Learning to teach. In L.S. Shulman & G. Sykes (Eds.), *Handbook of teaching and policy* (pp. 150–170). New York: Longman.

Feiman-Nemser, S., & Buchmann, M. (1985). Pitfalls of experience in teacher preparation. *Teachers College Record, 87*(1), 53–65.

Flower, L. (1981). *Problem-solving strategies for writing.* New York: Harcourt, Brace, Jovanovich.

Gere, A.R., et al. (1992). *Language and reflection: An integrated approach to teaching English.* New York: Macmillan.

Grossman, P.L. (1990). *The making of a teacher: Teacher knowledge and teacher education.* New York: Teachers College Press.

Grossman, P.L., & Richert, A.E. (1988). Unacknowledged knowledge growth: A re-examination of the effects of teacher education. *Teaching and Teacher Education, 4*(1), 53–62.

Gucker, P.C. (1966). *Essential English grammar.* New York: Dover.

Hayes, J.R., et al. (1992). *Reading empirical research studies: The rhetoric of research.* Hillsdale, NJ: Erlbaum.

Heath, S.B. (1983). *Ways with words.* New York: Cambridge University Press.

Hillocks, G., Jr. (1975). *Observing and writing.* Urbana, IL: National Council of Teachers of English.

Hillocks, G., Jr. (1986). *Research on written composition: New directions for teaching.* New York: National Conference on Research in English; Urbana, IL: Educational Resources Information Center.

Hillocks, G., Jr. (1994). Interpreting and counting: Objectivity in discourse analysis. In P. Smagorinsky (Ed.), *Speaking about writing: Reflections on research methodology* (pp. 183–204). Newbury Park, CA: Sage.

Hillocks, G., Jr., McCabe, B.J., McCampbell, J.F. (1971). *The dynamics of English instruction: Grades 7–12.* New York: Random House.

Hook, J.N., & Evans, W.H. (1982). *The teaching of high school English.* 4th ed. New York: Wiley.

Hynds, S., & Rubin, D.L. (Eds.). (1990). *Perspectives on talk and learning.* Urbana, IL: National Council of Teachers of English.

Johannessen, L., Kahn, E., & Walter, C. (1982). *Designing and sequencing prewriting activities.* Urbana, IL: National Council of Teachers of English.

Kaestle, C.F. (1983). *Pillars of the republic: Common schools and the American society, 1780–1860.* New York: Hill and Wang.

Kahn, E., Walter, C., & Johannnessen, L. (1984). *Writing about literature.* Urbana, IL: National Council of Teachers of English.

Kirby, D., Liner, T., & Vinz, R. (1988). *Inside out: Developmental strategies for teaching writing.* Portsmouth, NH: Boynton/Cook-Heinemann.

Lampert, M. (1984). Teaching about thinking and thinking about teaching. *Journal of Curriculum Studies, 16*(1), 1–18.

Lindemann, E. (1982). *A rhetoric for writing teachers.* New York: Oxford University Press.

Lortie, D. (1975). *Schoolteacher: A sociological study.* Chicago: University of Chicago Press.

Marshall, J.D., Smagorinsky, P., & Smith, M.W. (1995). *The language of interpretation: Patterns of discourse in discussions of literature.* NCTE Research Report No. 27. Urbana, IL: National Council of Teachers of English.

McCarthey, S.J., & Raphael, T.E. (1992). Alternative research perspectives. In J.W. Irwin & M.A. Doyle (Eds.), *Reading/Writing Connections: Learning from research* (pp. 2–30). Newark, DE: International Reading Association.

Murray, D.M. (1984). *Write to learn.* New York: Holt, Rinehart & Winston.

North, S.P. (1987). *The making of knowledge in composition.* Portsmouth, NH: Boynton/Cook-Heinemann.

Perl, S., & Wilson, N. (1986). *Through teachers' eyes.* Portsmouth, NH: Heinemann.

Piaget, J. (1977). *The development of thought: Equilibration of cognitive structures.* New York: Viking.

Pooley, R. (1974). *Teaching English usage.* Urbana, IL: National Council of Teachers of English.

Probst, R. (1984). *Adolescent literature: Response and analysis.* Columbus, OH: Merrill.

Purves, A., Rogers, T., & Soter, A. (1990). *How porcupines make love II: Teaching a response-centered literature curriculum.* New York: Longman.

Rosenblatt, L.M. (1938). *Literature as exploration.* New York: Appleton-Century.

Rosenblatt, L.M. (1978). *The reader, the text, the poem: The transactional theory of the literary work.* Carbondale, IL: Southern Illinois University Press.

Rubin, D.L., & Dodd, W.M. (1985). *Talking into writing: Exercises for basic writers.* Urbana, IL: National Council of Teachers of English.

Shaughnessy, M.P. (1977). *Errors and expectations: A guide for the teacher of basic writing.* New York: Oxford University Press.

Sheridan, D. (1993). *Teaching secondary English: Readings and applications.* New York: Longman.

Smagorinsky, P. (1986). An apology for structured composition instruction. *Written Communication, 3*(1), 105–122.

Smagorinsky, P. (1987). Graves revisited: A look at the methods and conclusions of the New Hampshire study. *Written Communication, 4*(4), 331–342.

Smagorinsky, P. (1992). Towards a civic education in a multicultural society: Ethical problems in teaching literature. *English Education, 24*(4), 212–228.

Smagorinsky, P. (In press). New canons, new problems: Promoting a sense of kinship among students of diversity. In B.A. Goebel & J. Hall (Eds.), *Teaching the new canon: Students, teachers, and texts in the multicultural classroom.* Urbana, IL: National Council of Teachers of English.

Smagorinsky, P., & Fly, P.K. (1993). The social environment of the classroom: A Vygotskian perspective on small group process. *Communication Education, 42*(2), 159–171).

Smagorinsky, P., & Gevinson, S. (1989). *Fostering the reader's response: Rethinking the literature curriculum, grades 7–12.* Palo Alto, CA: Dale Seymour.

Smagorinsky, P., & Jordahl, A. (1991). The student teacher/cooperating teacher collaborative study: A new source of knowledge. *English Education, 23*(1), 54–59.

Smagorinsky, P., McCann, T., & Kern, S. (1987). *Explorations: Introductory activities for literature and composition, grades 7–12.* Urbana, IL: National Council of Teachers of English.

Small, R., & Strzepek, J. (1988). *A casebook for English teachers.* Belmont, CA: Wadsworth.

Smith, M.W. (1991). *Understanding unreliable narrators: Reading between the lines in the literature classroom:* Urbana, IL: National Council of Teachers of English.

Strong, W. (1987). *Creative approaches to sentence combining.* Urbana, IL: National Council of Teachers of English.

Stryker, D. (Ed.). (1967). *Method in the teaching of English.* Champaign, IL: National Council of Teachers of English.

Tabachnick, B.R., & Zeichner, K.M. (1984). The impact of the student teaching experiences on the development of teacher perspectives. *Journal of Teacher Education, 35*(6), 28–42.

Tchudi, S.N. (1990). *Planning and assessing the curriculum in English language arts.* Alexandria, VA: Association for Supervision and Curriculum Development.

Tchudi, S.N., & Mitchell, D. (1989). *Explorations in the teaching of English.* 3rd ed. New York: HarperCollins.

Tchudi, S.N., & Tchudi, S.J. (1991). *The English/language arts handbook: Classroom strategies for teachers.* Rev. ed. Portsmouth, NH: Boynton/Cook.

Tyack, D.B. (1974). *The one best system: A history of American urban education.* Cambridge, MA: Harvard University Press.

Tyler, R. (1949). *Basic principles of curriculum and instruction.* Chicago: University of Chicago Press.

Vygotsky, L. (1978). *Mind in society: The development of higher psychological processes.* M. Cole, V. John-Steiner, S. Scribner, & E. Souberman (Eds.). Cambridge, MA: Harvard University Press.

Vygotsky, L. (1986). *Thought and Language.* Cambridge, MA: MIT Press.

Weaver, C. (1979). *Grammar for teachers: Perspectives and definitions.* Urbana, IL: National Council of Teachers of English.

Wolfe, D., chair, and the NCTE Standing Committee on Teacher Preparation and Certification. (1986). *Guidelines for the preparation of teachers of English language arts.* Urbana, IL: National Council of Teachers of English.

Zeichner, K.M. (1988). Understanding the character and quality of the academic and professional components of teacher education. Paper presented at the annual meeting of the American Educational Research Association, New Orleans. April.

Index

Authors

Peter Smagorinsky teaches undergraduate and graduate courses in English education at the University of Oklahoma. He originally learned about teaching in the MAT program at the University of Chicago, developed his ideas as a high school English teacher in the Chicago area from 1977 through 1990, and received his Ph.D. in English education from the University of Chicago in 1989. He has published a number of works concerning the theory, research, and practice of the teaching of English. Recent books include *Speaking about Writing: Reflections on Research Methodology* (1994) and *The Language of Interpretation: Patterns of Discourse in Discussions of Literature* (1995). He has also published articles in *English Education, English Journal, Oklahoma English Journal, Research in the Teaching of English, Review of Educational Research, Written Communication,* and other journals. He is a member of the Executive Committee of the Oklahoma Council of Teachers of English and NCTE's Standing Committee on Research.

Melissa E. Whiting taught high school English and ESL in Oklahoma for ten years. She received her B.A. and M.A. from the University of Tulsa and is currently a doctoral student in English education at the University of Oklahoma. At the University of Oklahoma, she has worked as a research assistant on several projects, supervised student teachers, and tutored students in the Athletic Academic Center. She has published articles in *GED Items, Oklahoma English Journal,* and *English Journal,* and made presentations to the American Educational Research Association, the Association of Teachers of English Grammar, the National Council of Teachers of English, and the Quality Schools Conference. She has also worked as a consultant for the advanced placement exam and the GED.